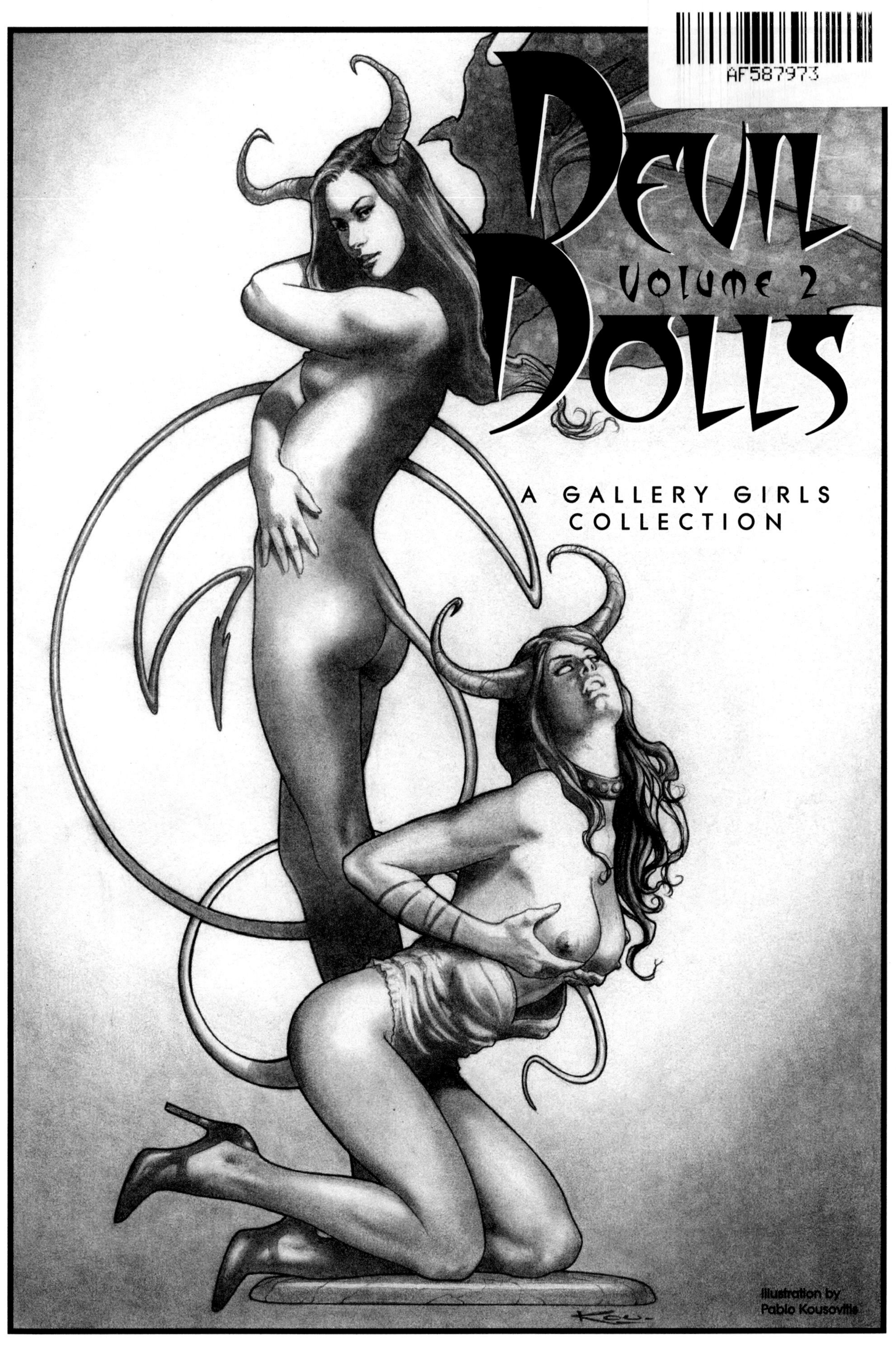

AN SQP PRESENTATION

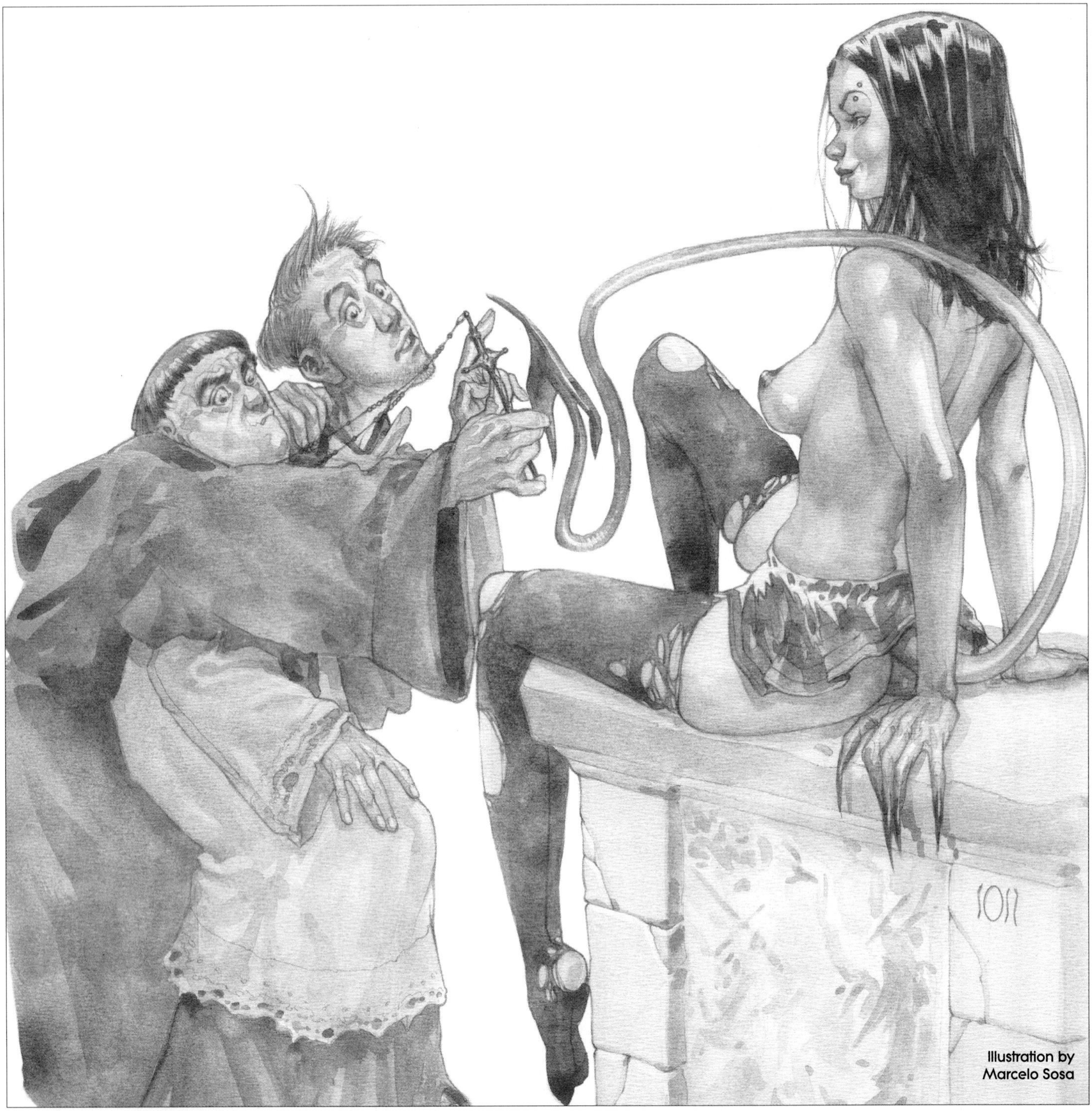

Illustration by
Marcelo Sosa

DEVIL DOLLS

Volume Two

 Printed in China.
Book design by Grassy Knoll Studios.

Published by
SQP Inc.
PO Box 248 - Columbus, NJ 08022

Sal Quartuccio & Bob Keenan - Publishers

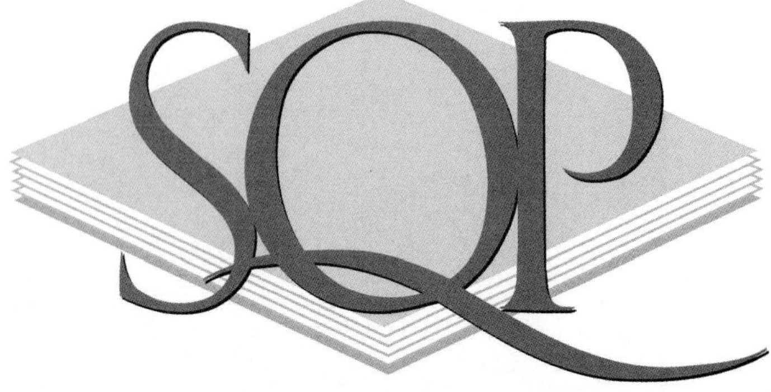

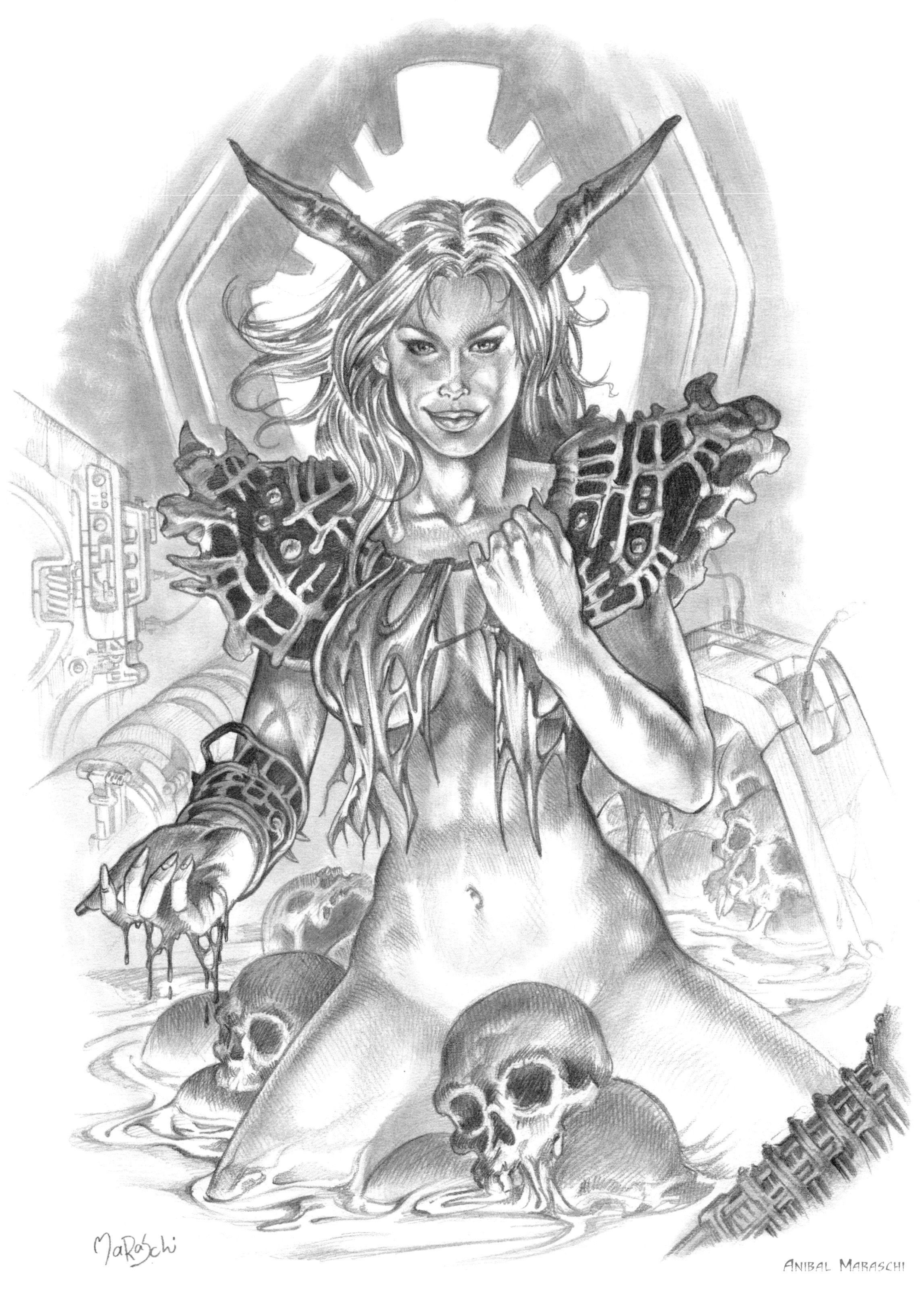
Maraschi
Anibal Maraschi

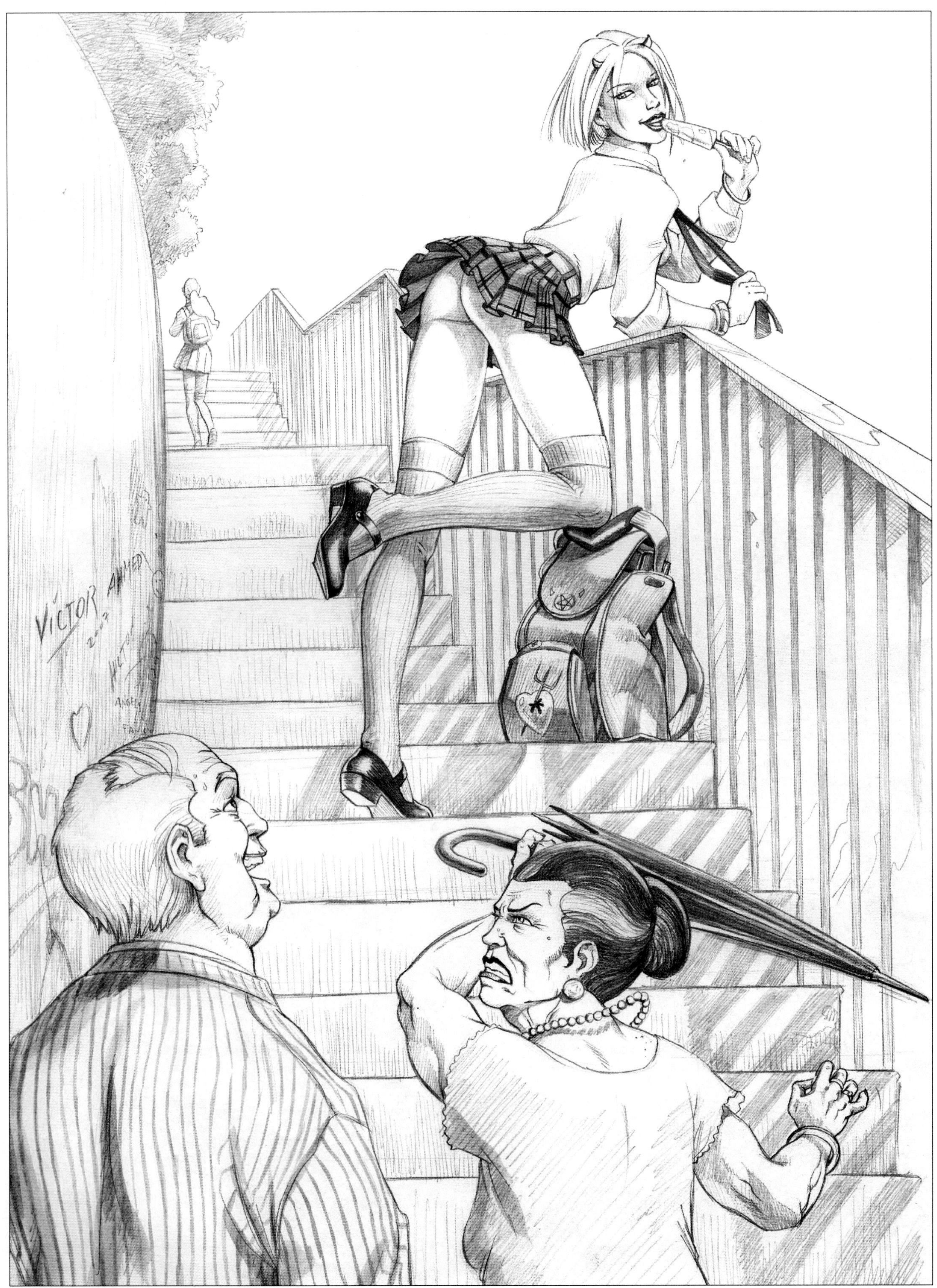

VICTOR AHMED

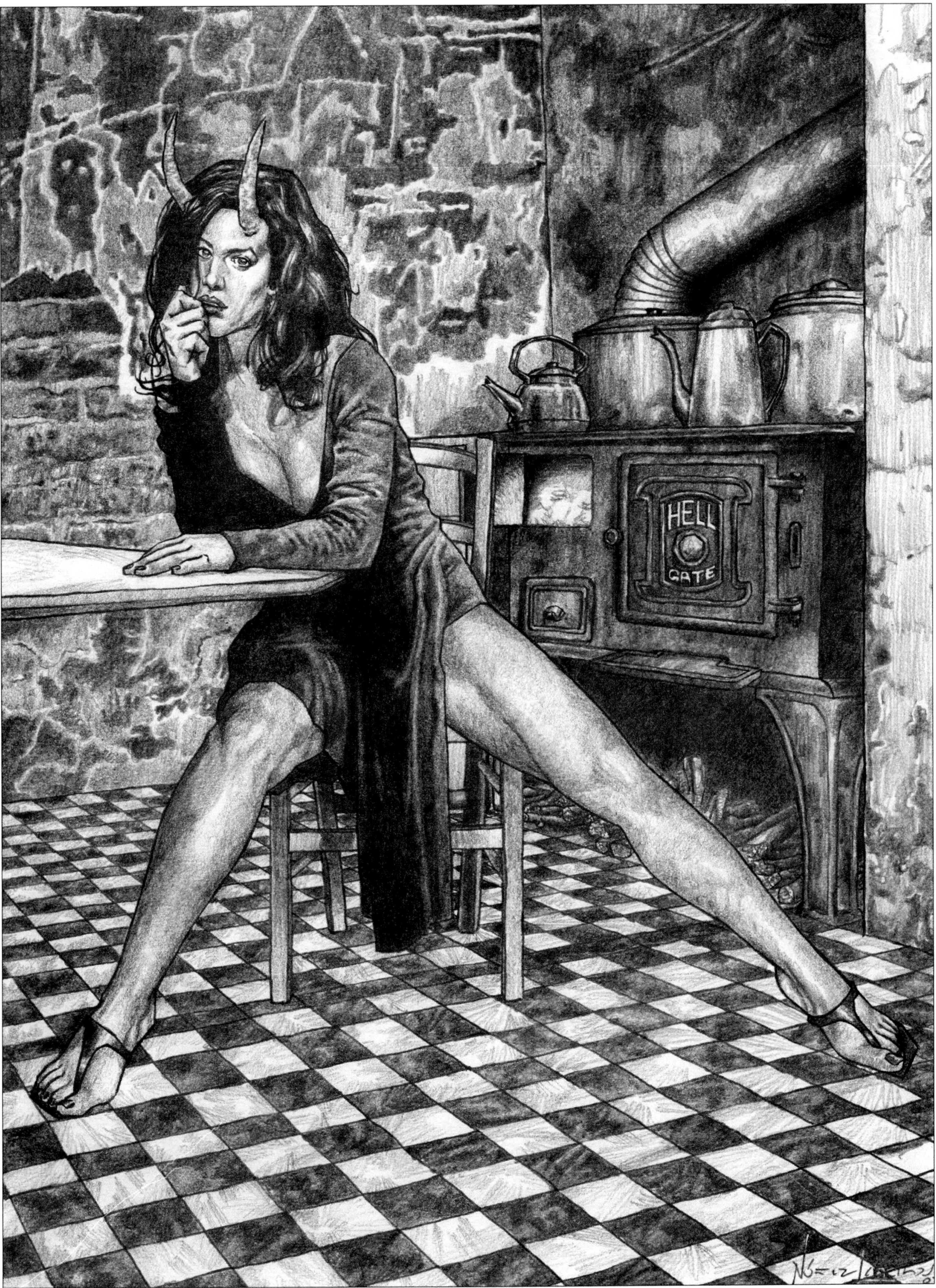

Juan Lencina

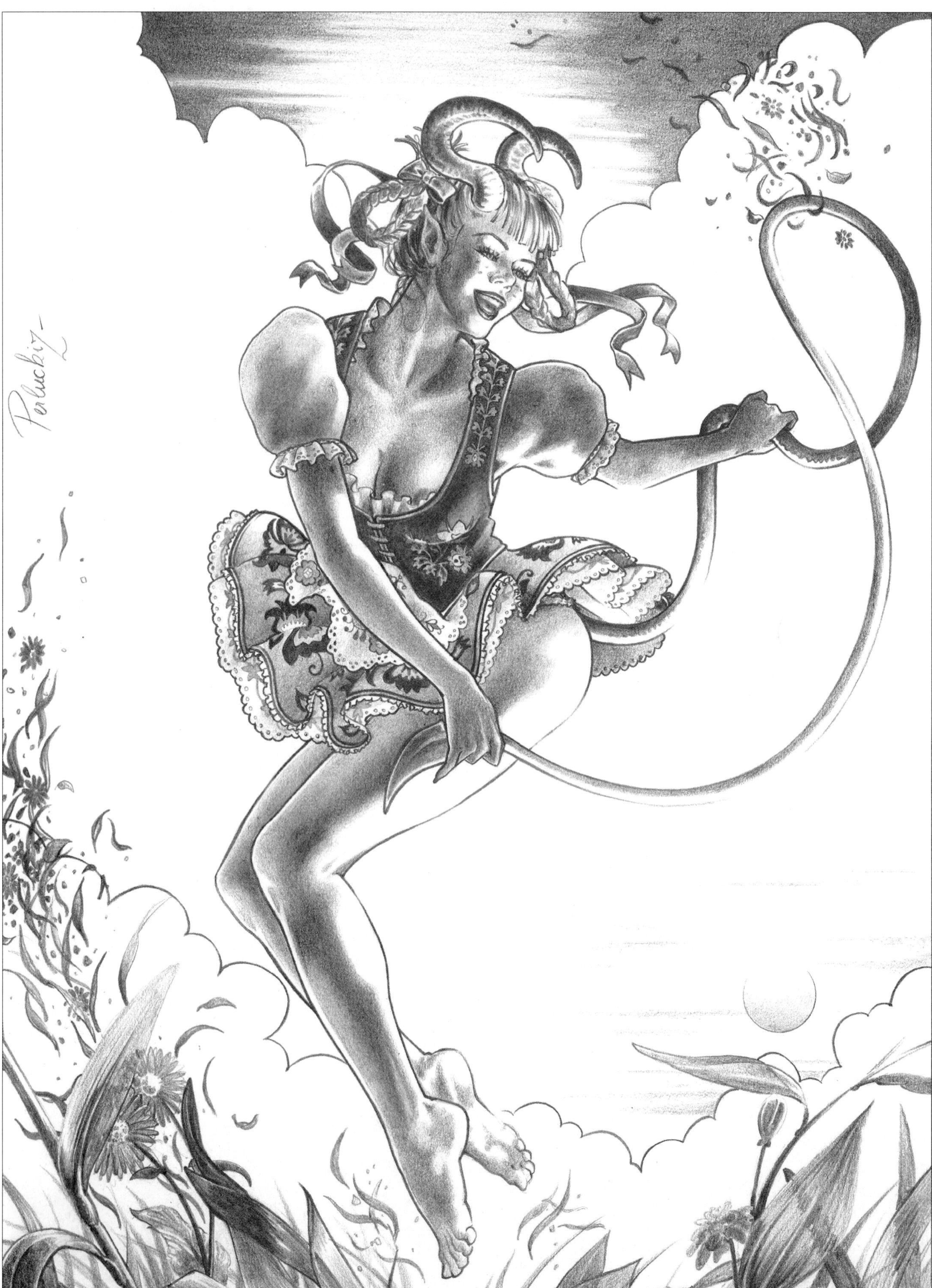

Perla Pilucki

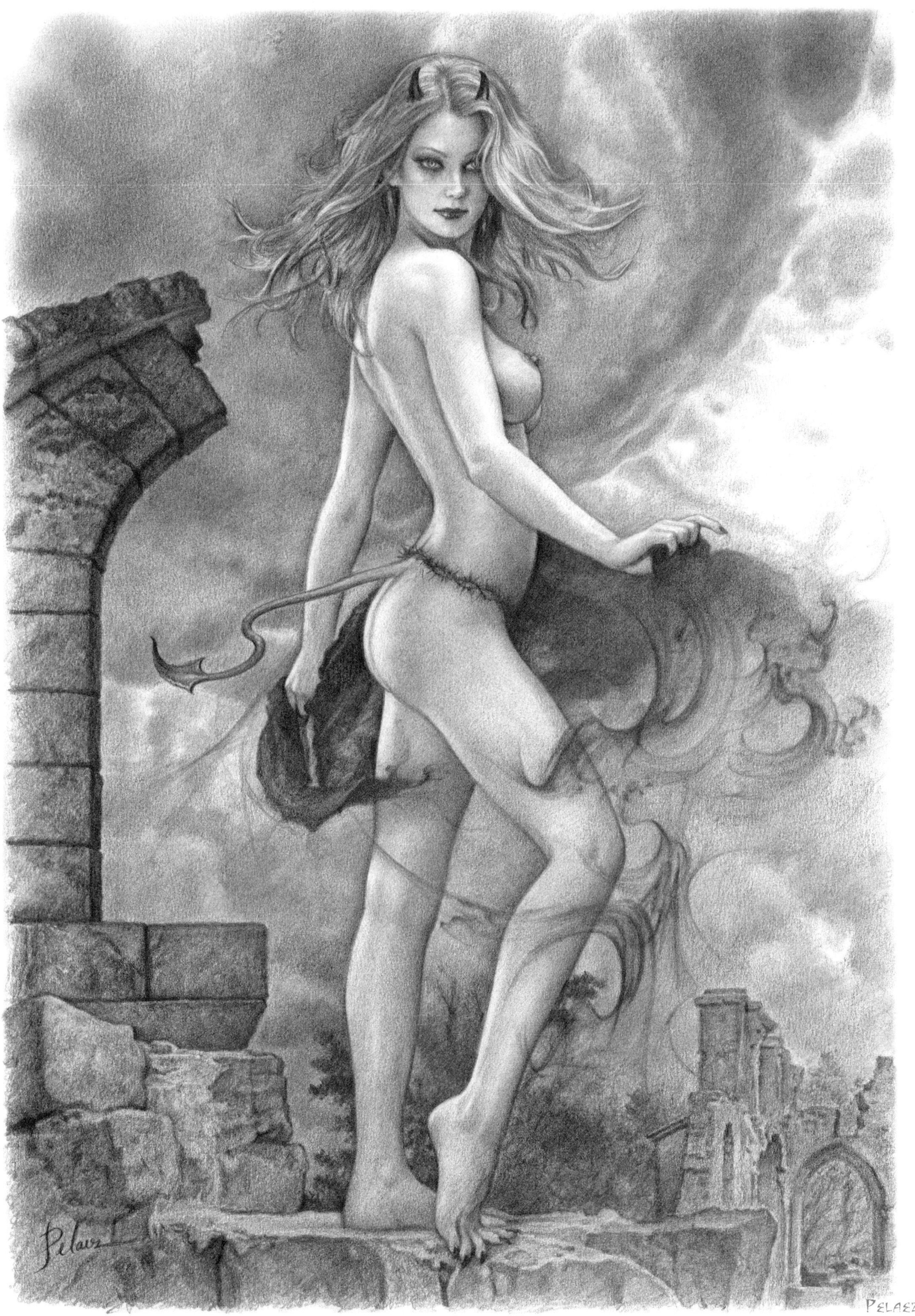

PELAEZ

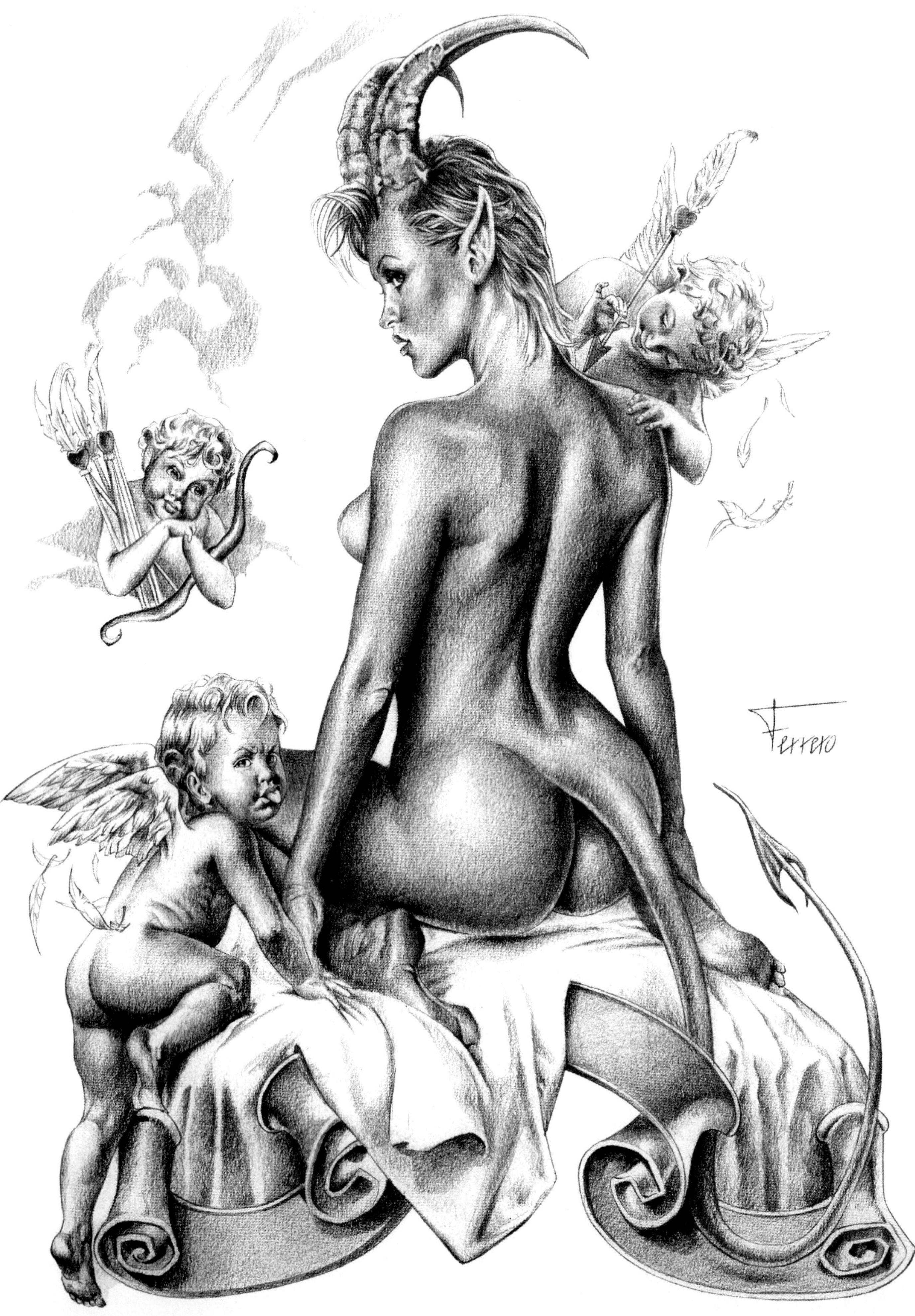

ALEJANDRO FERRERO

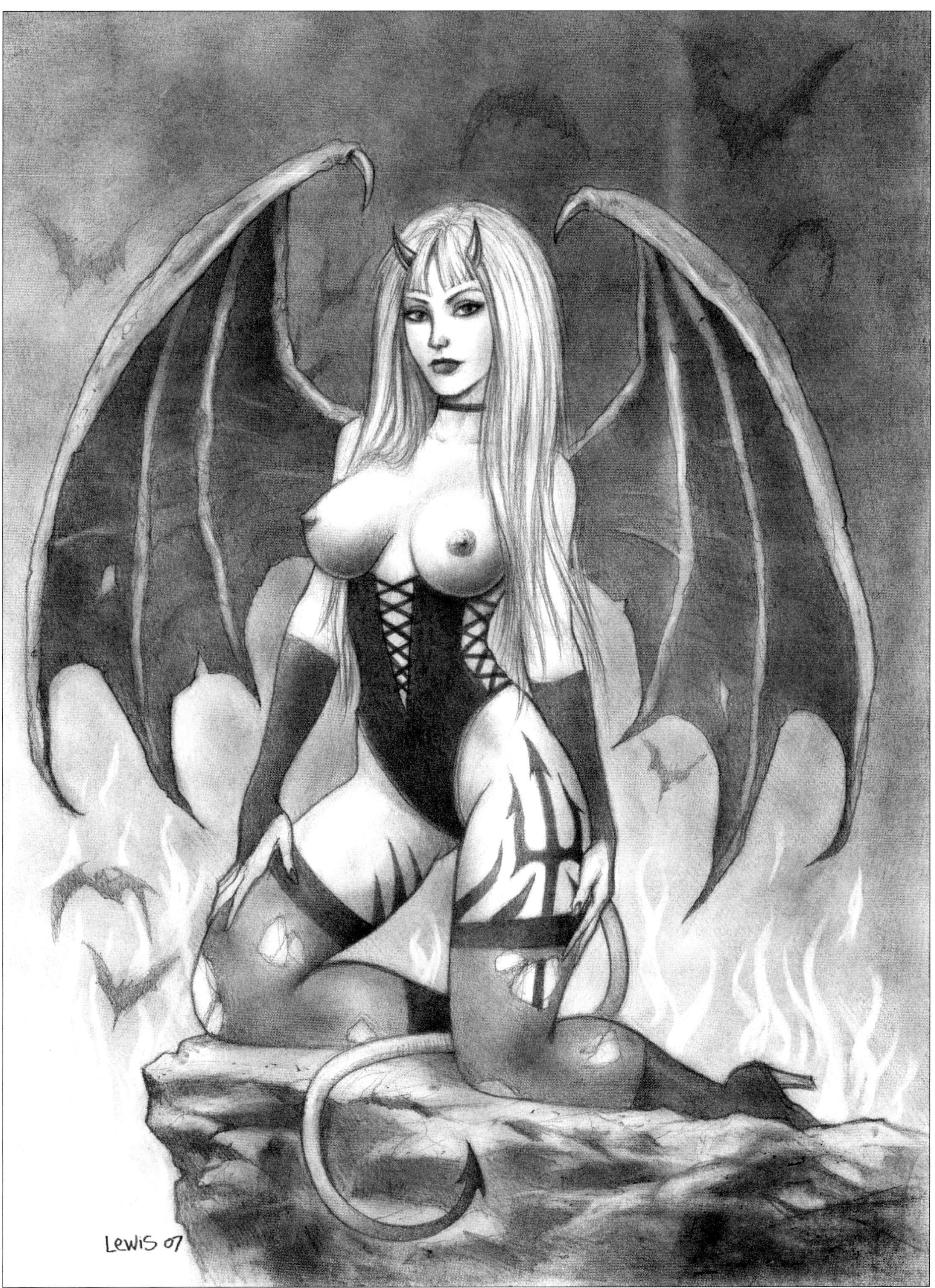

SCOTT LEWIS

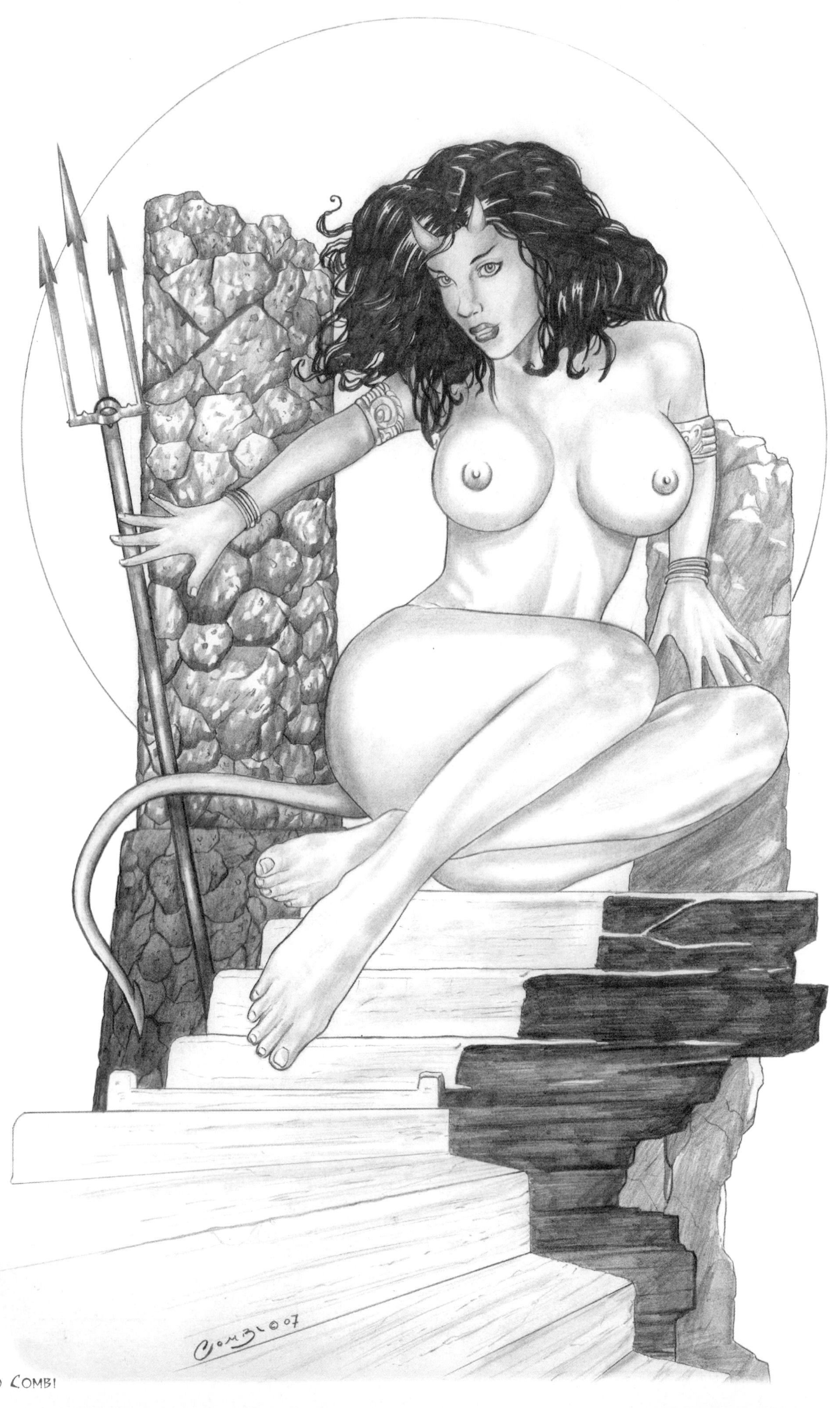

Federico Combi

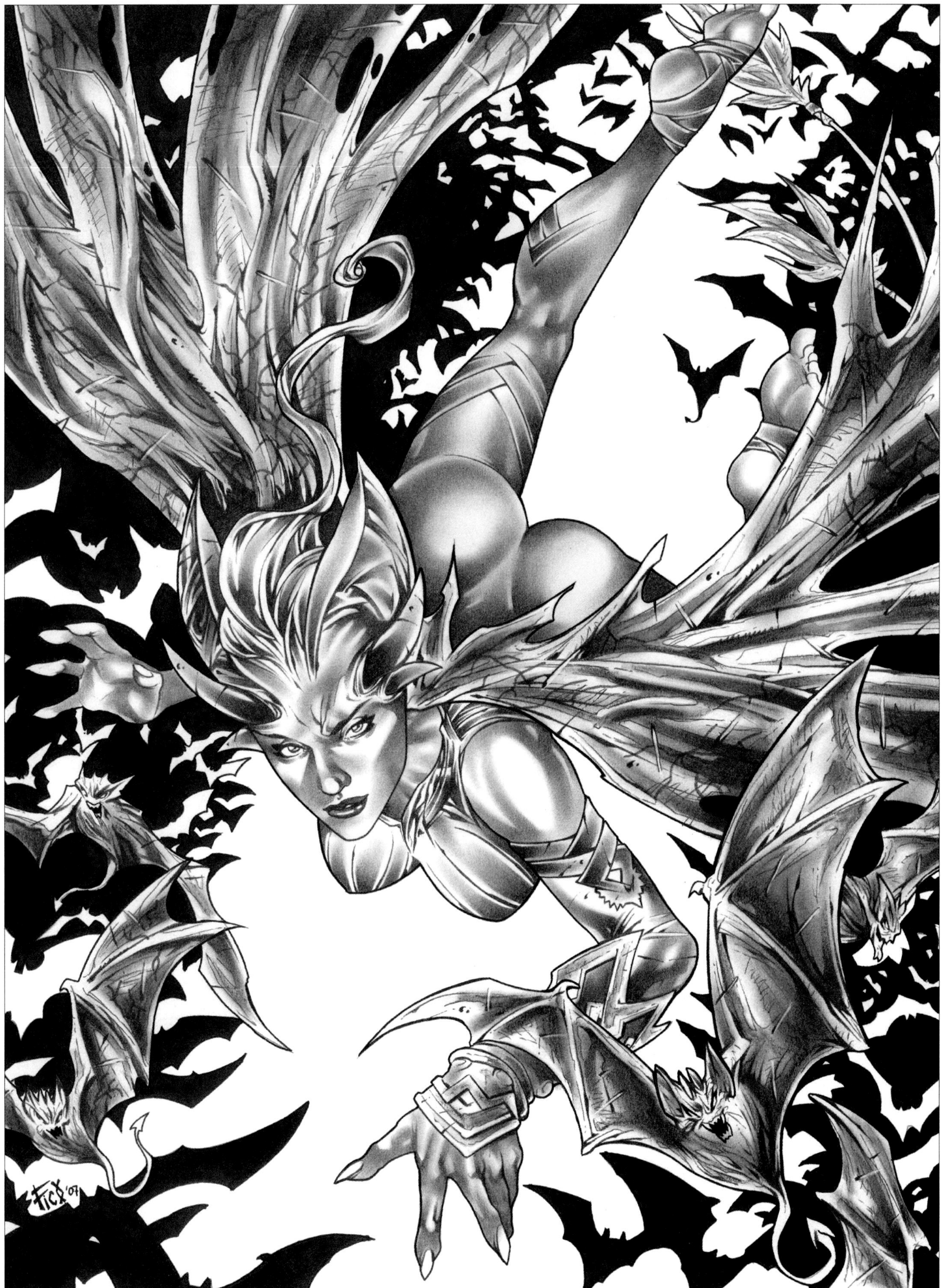

Federico Ossio

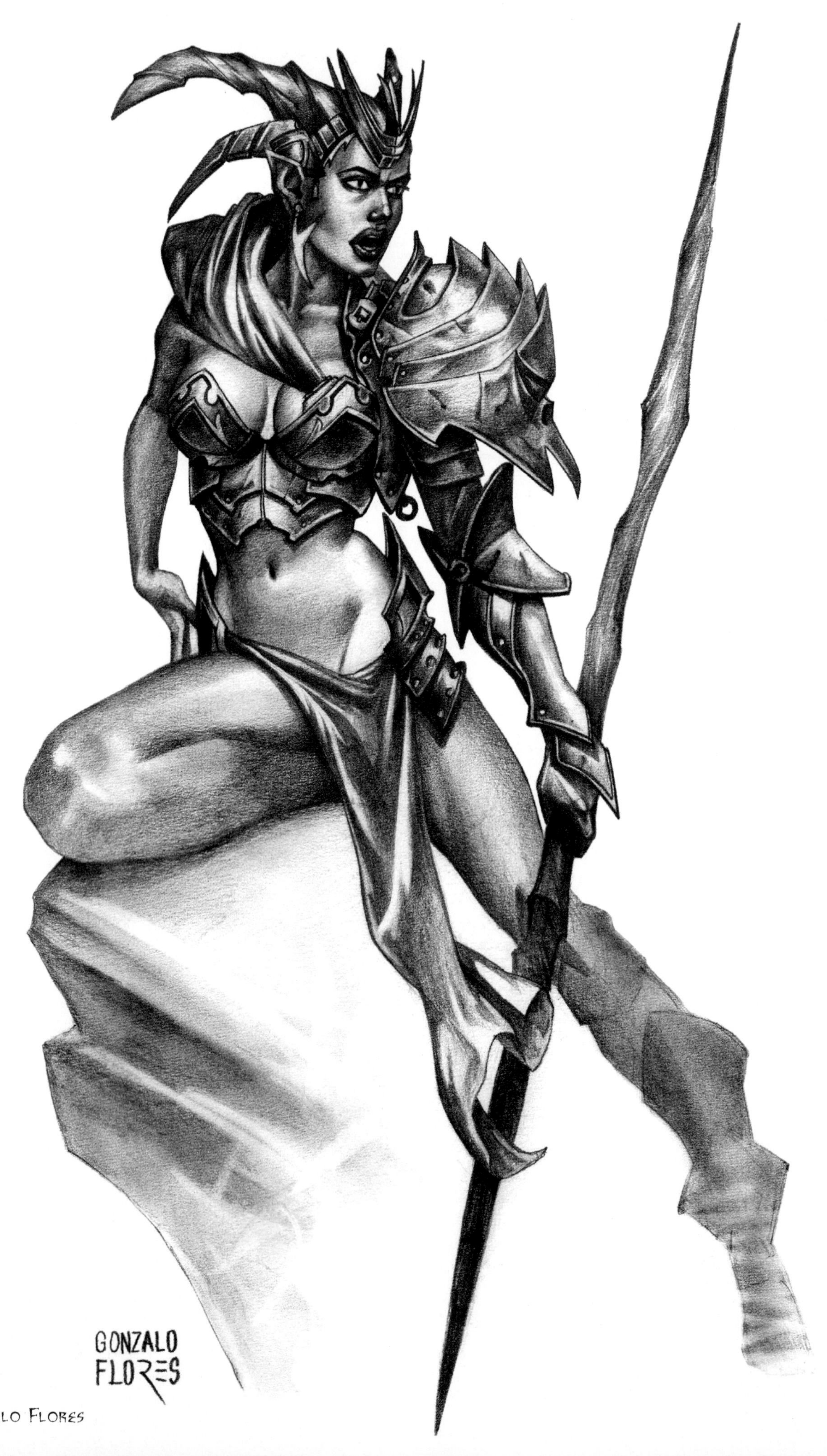

Gonzalo Flores

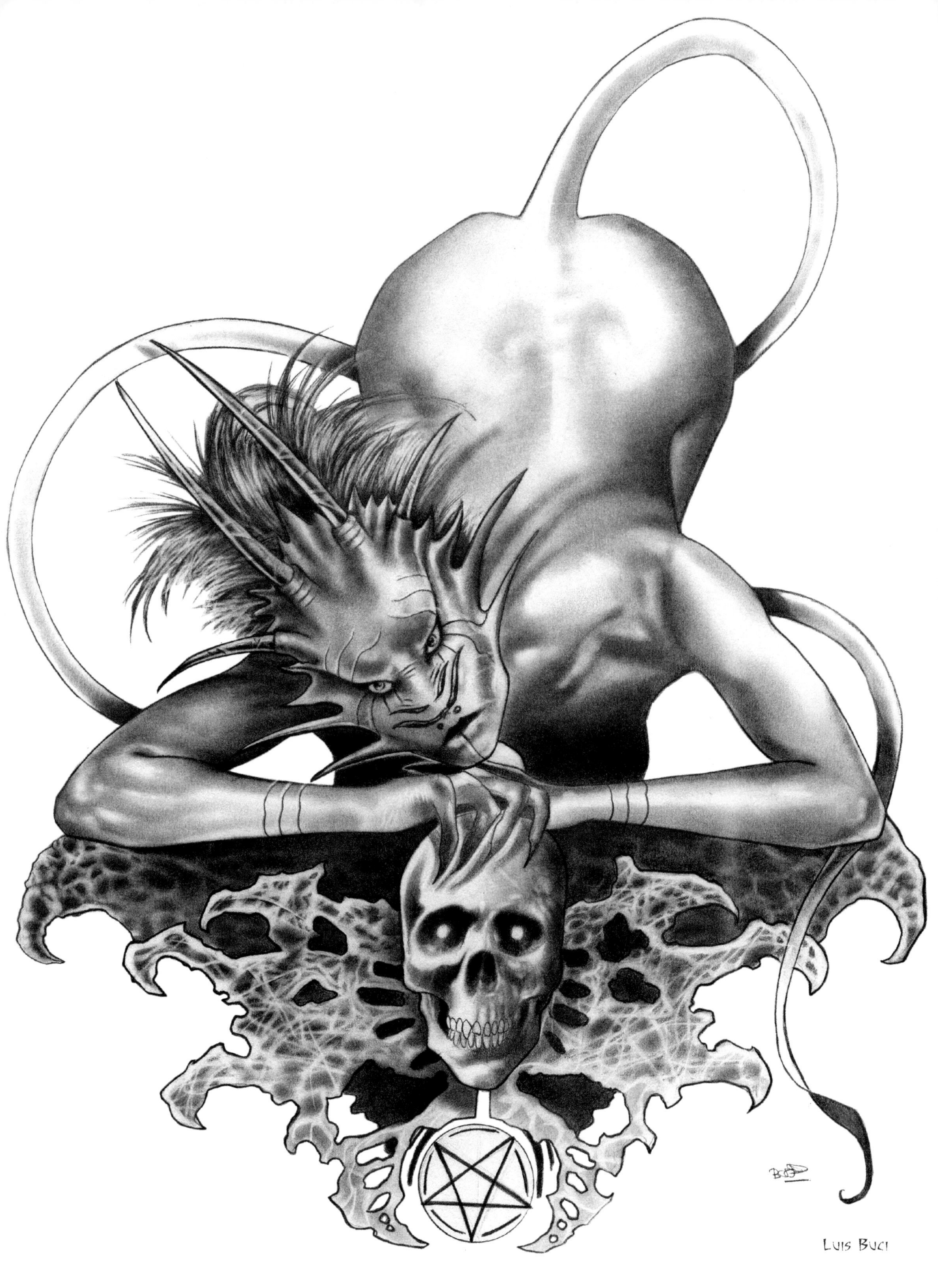
Luis Buci

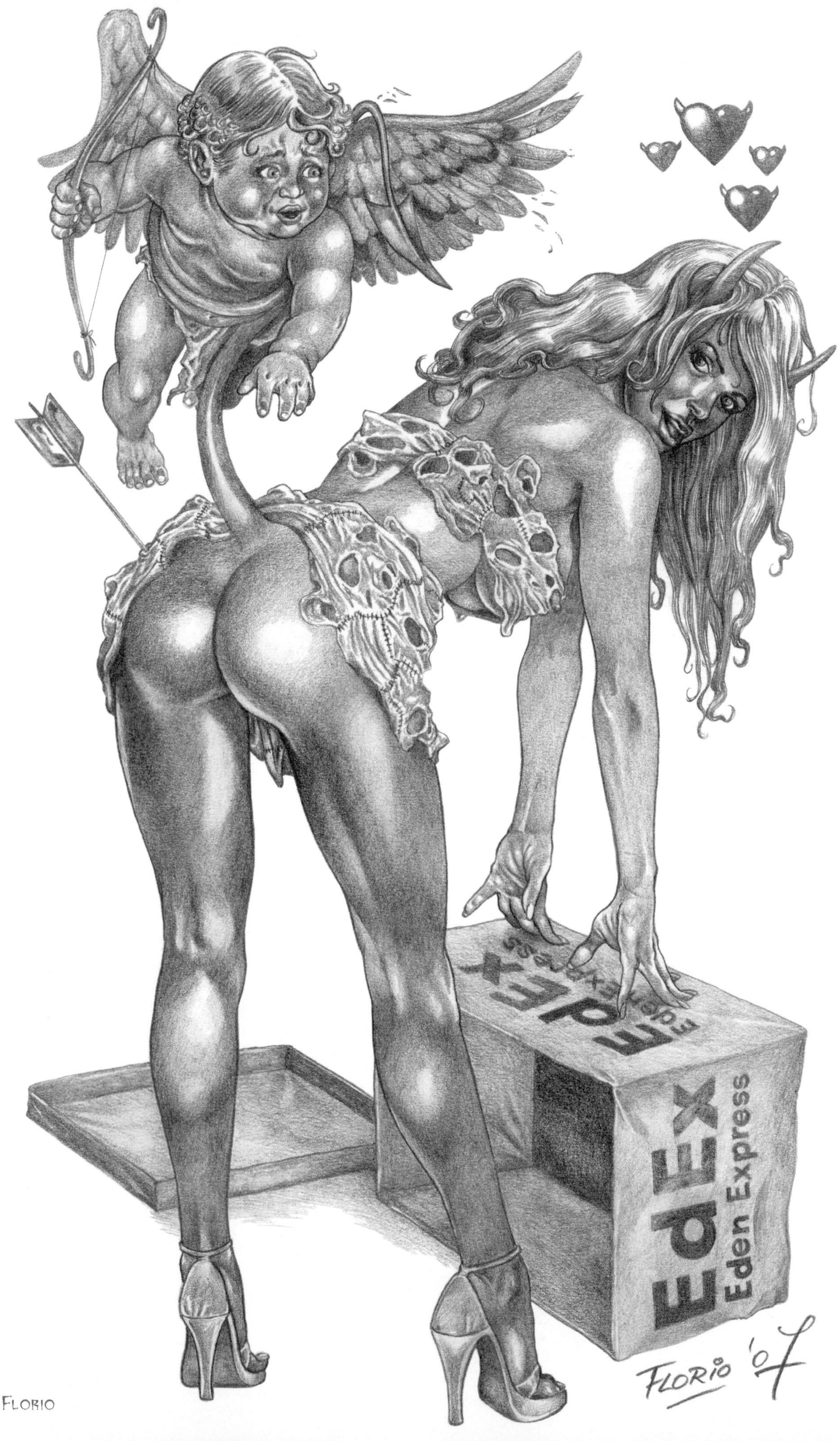

Diego Florio

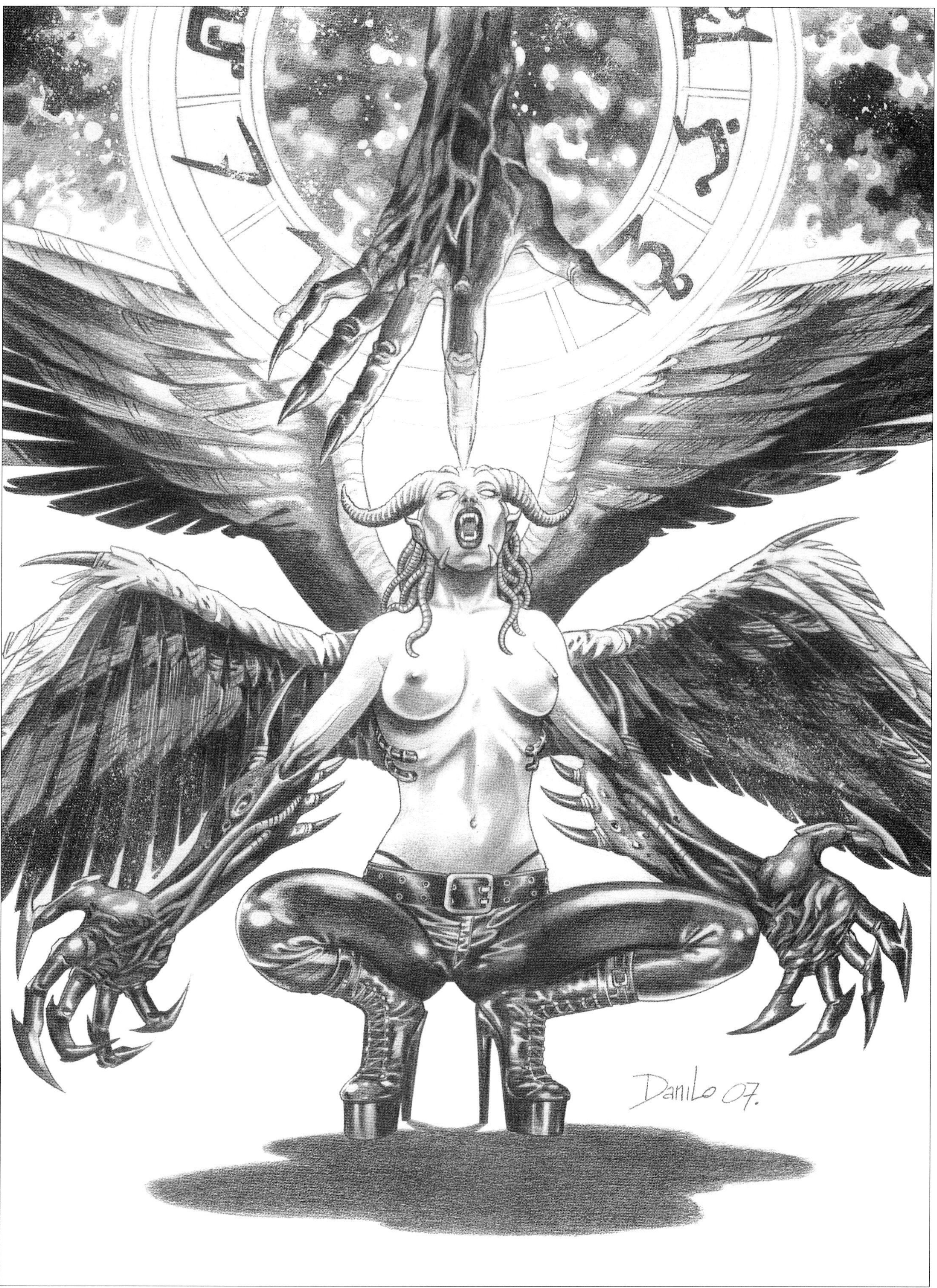

DANILO GUIDA

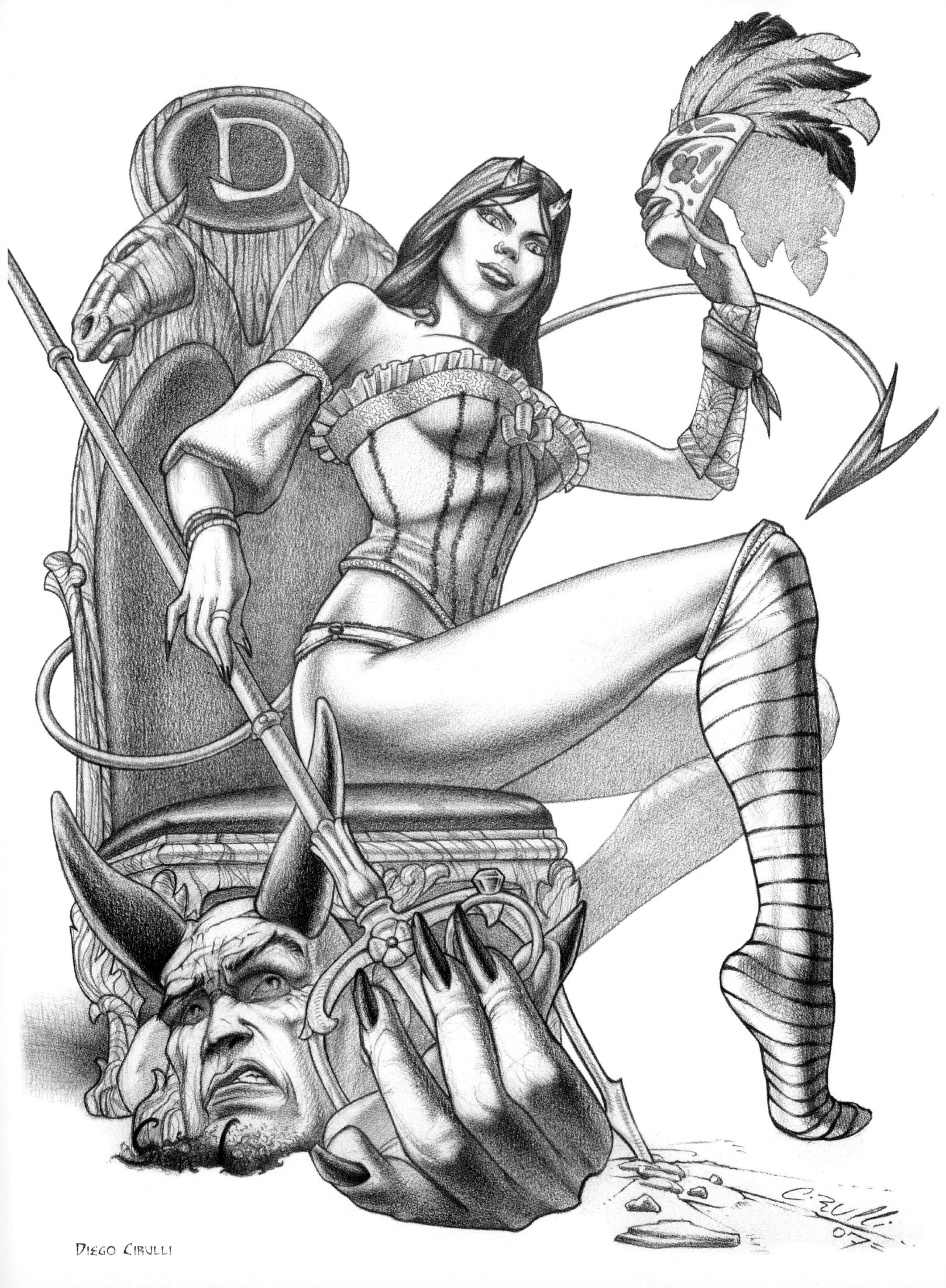
Diego Cirulli

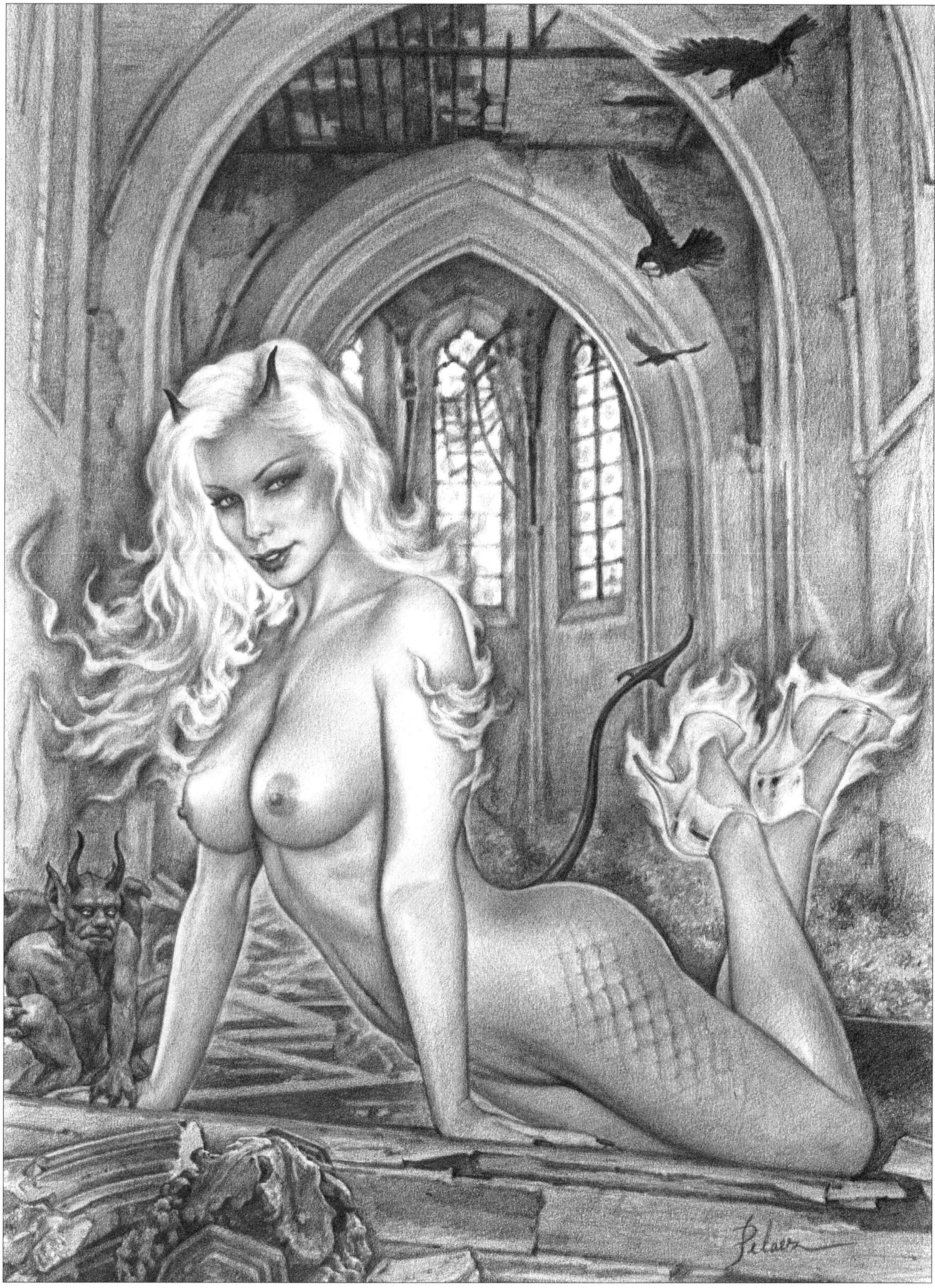

PELAEZ

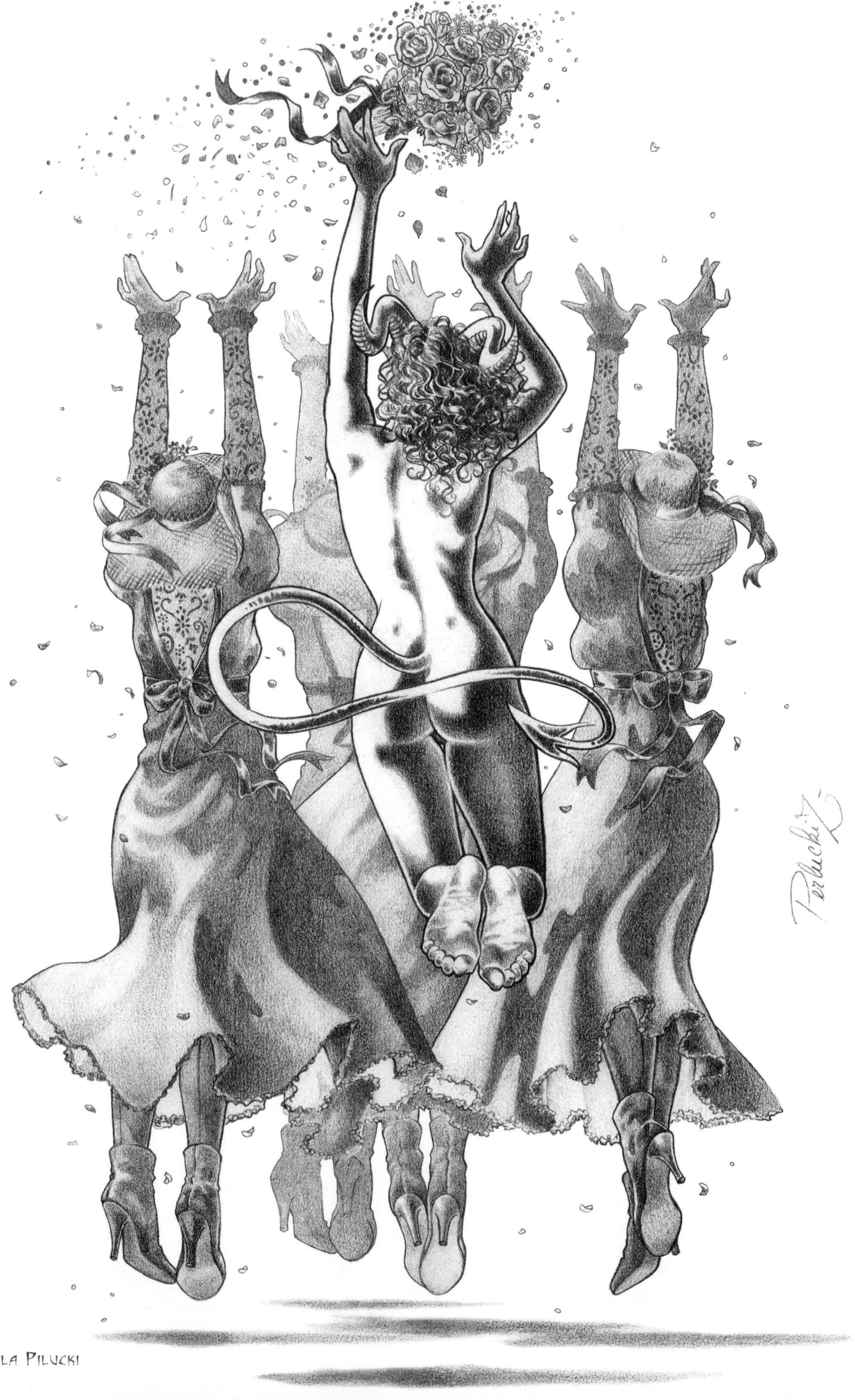
Perla Pilucki

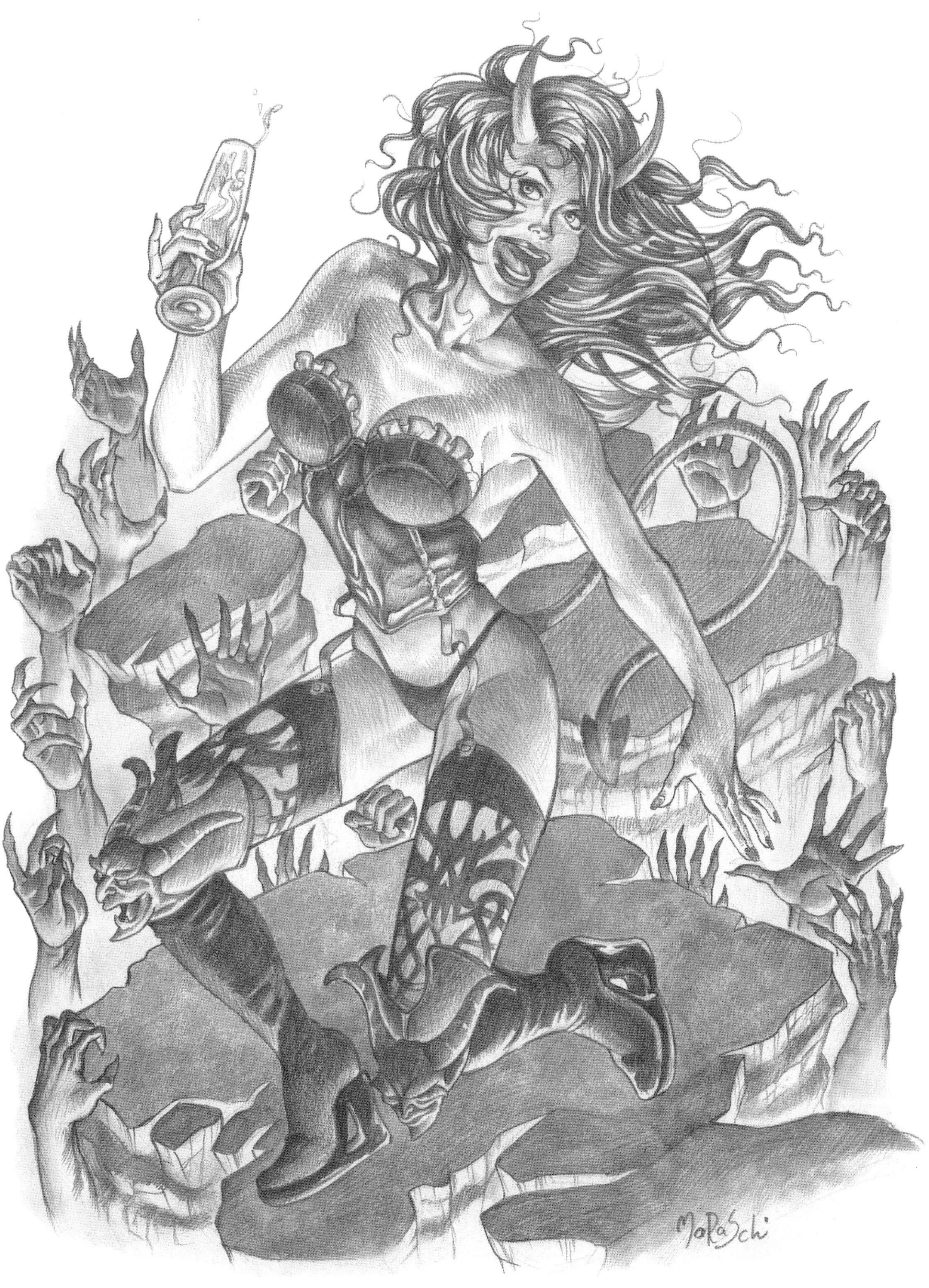

Anibal Maraschi

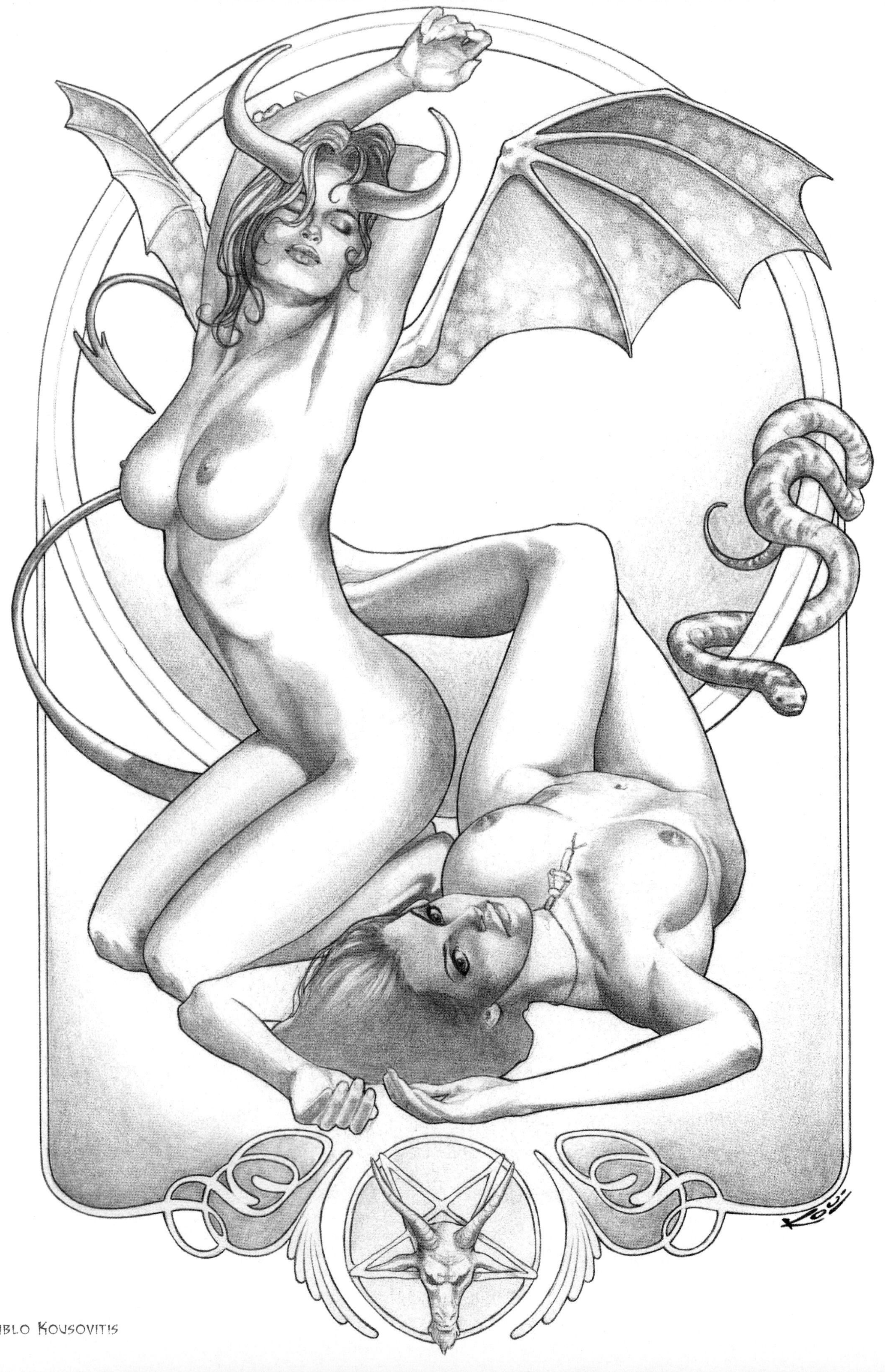

Pablo Kousovitis

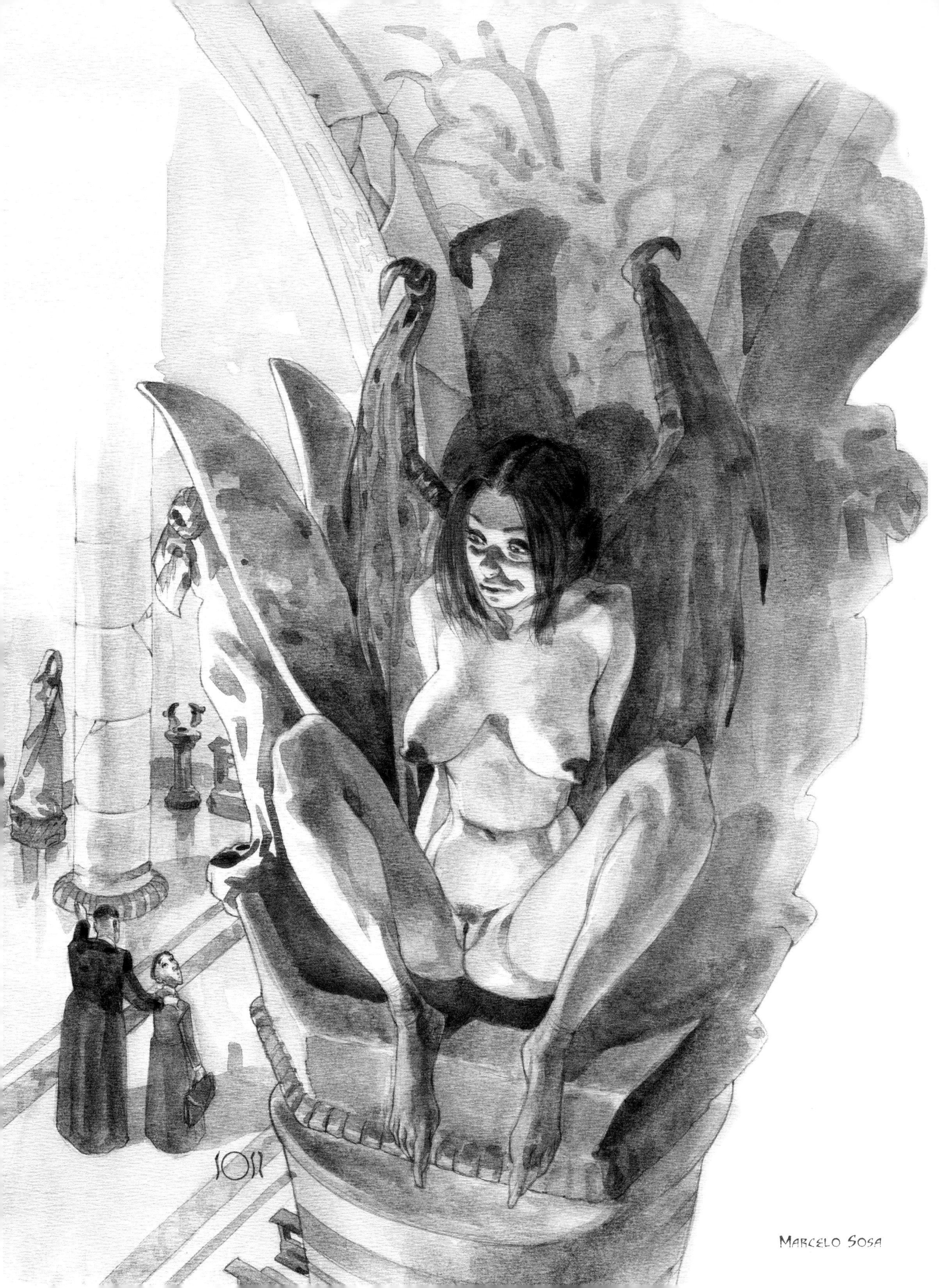
MARCELO SOSA

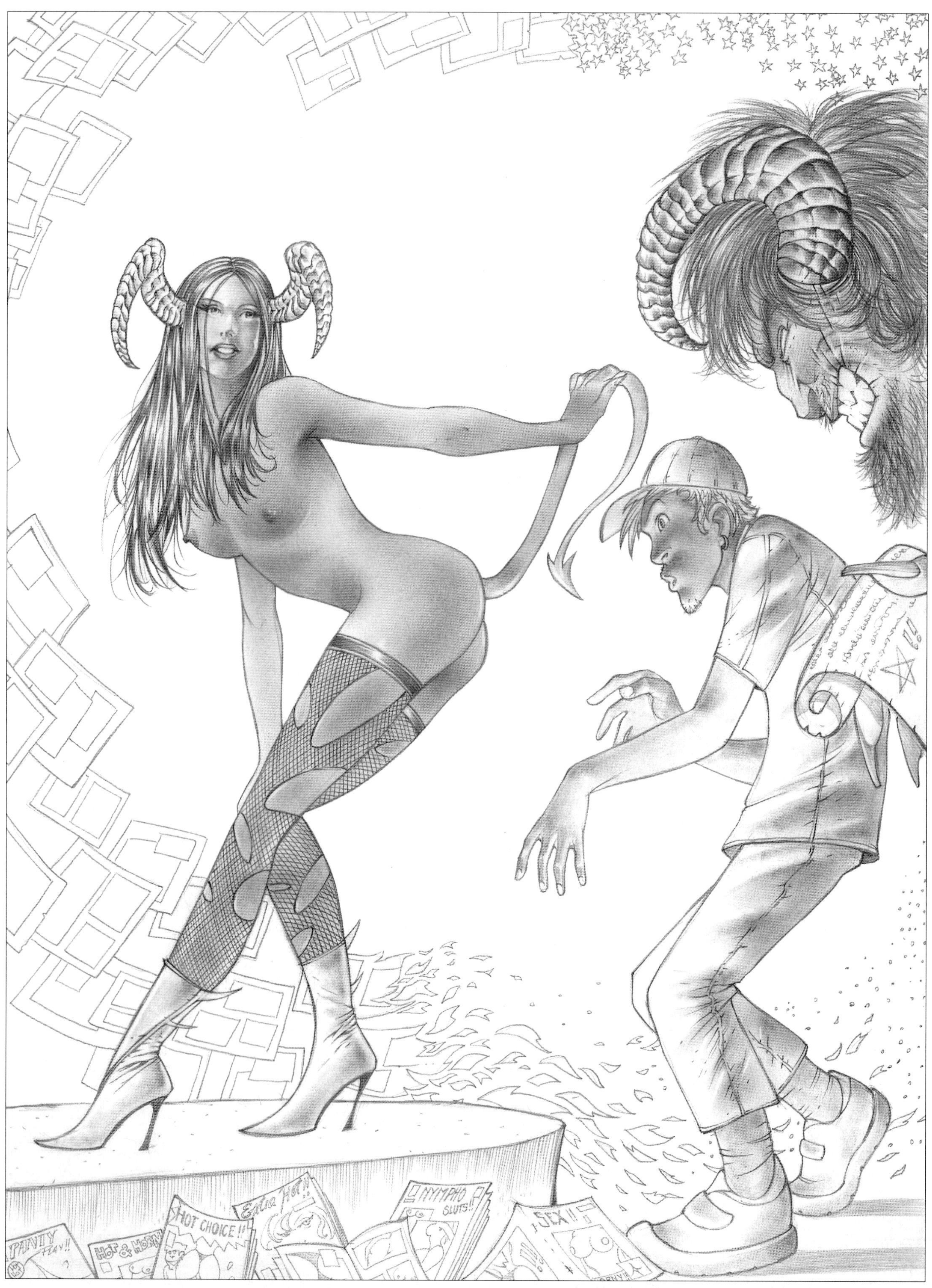

J.L. CZERNIAWSKI

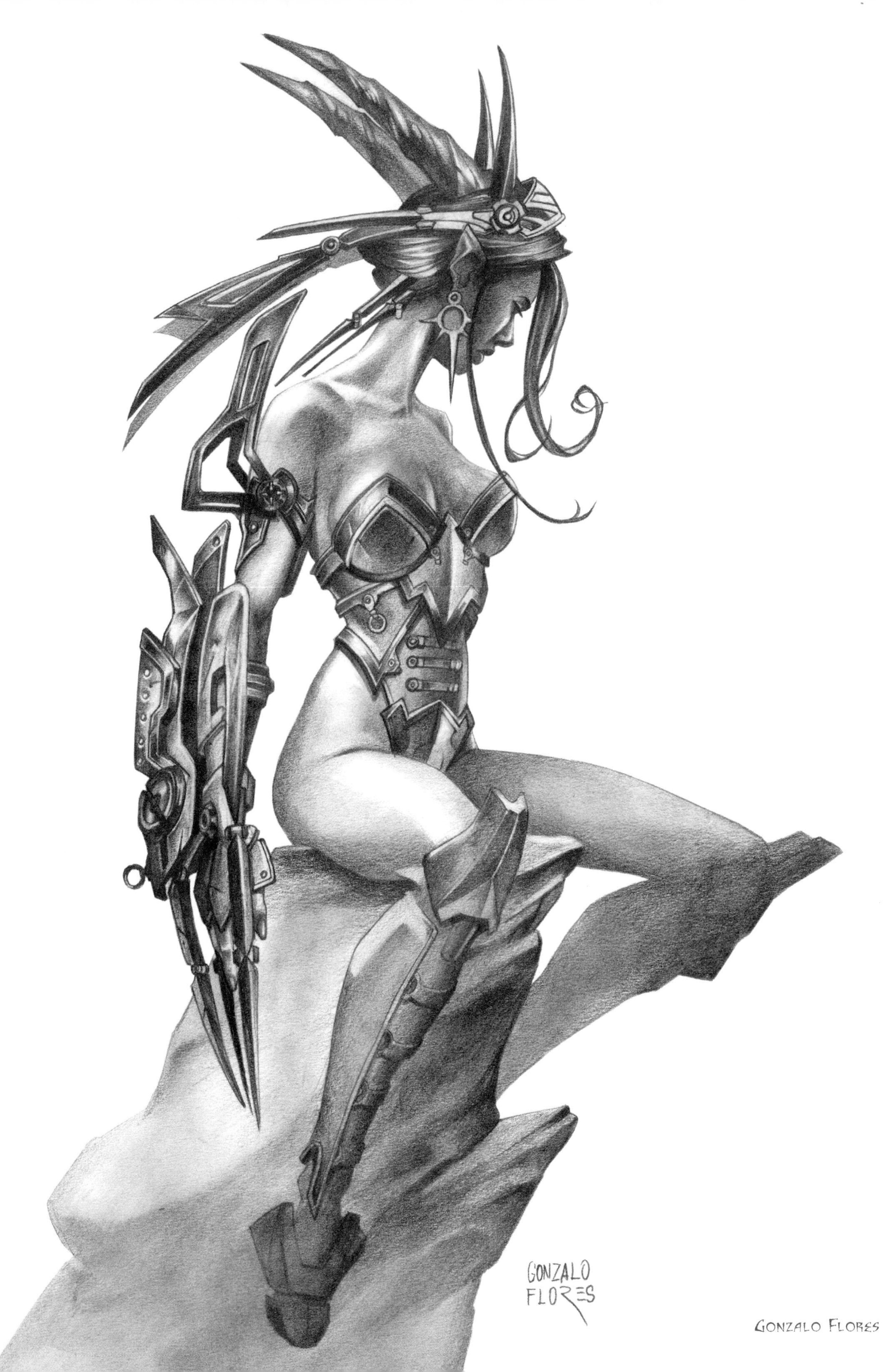

GONZALO FLORES

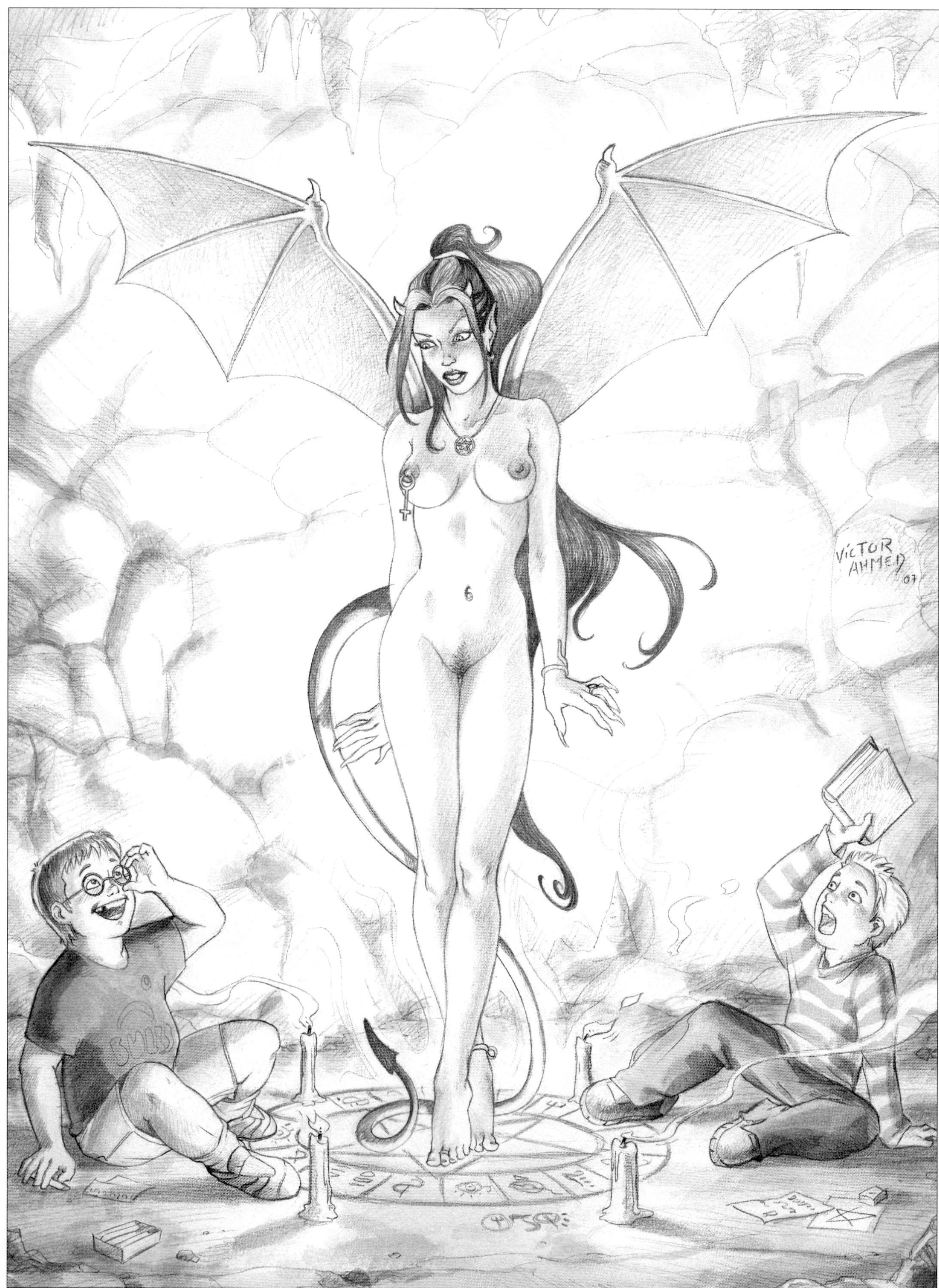

Victor Ahmed

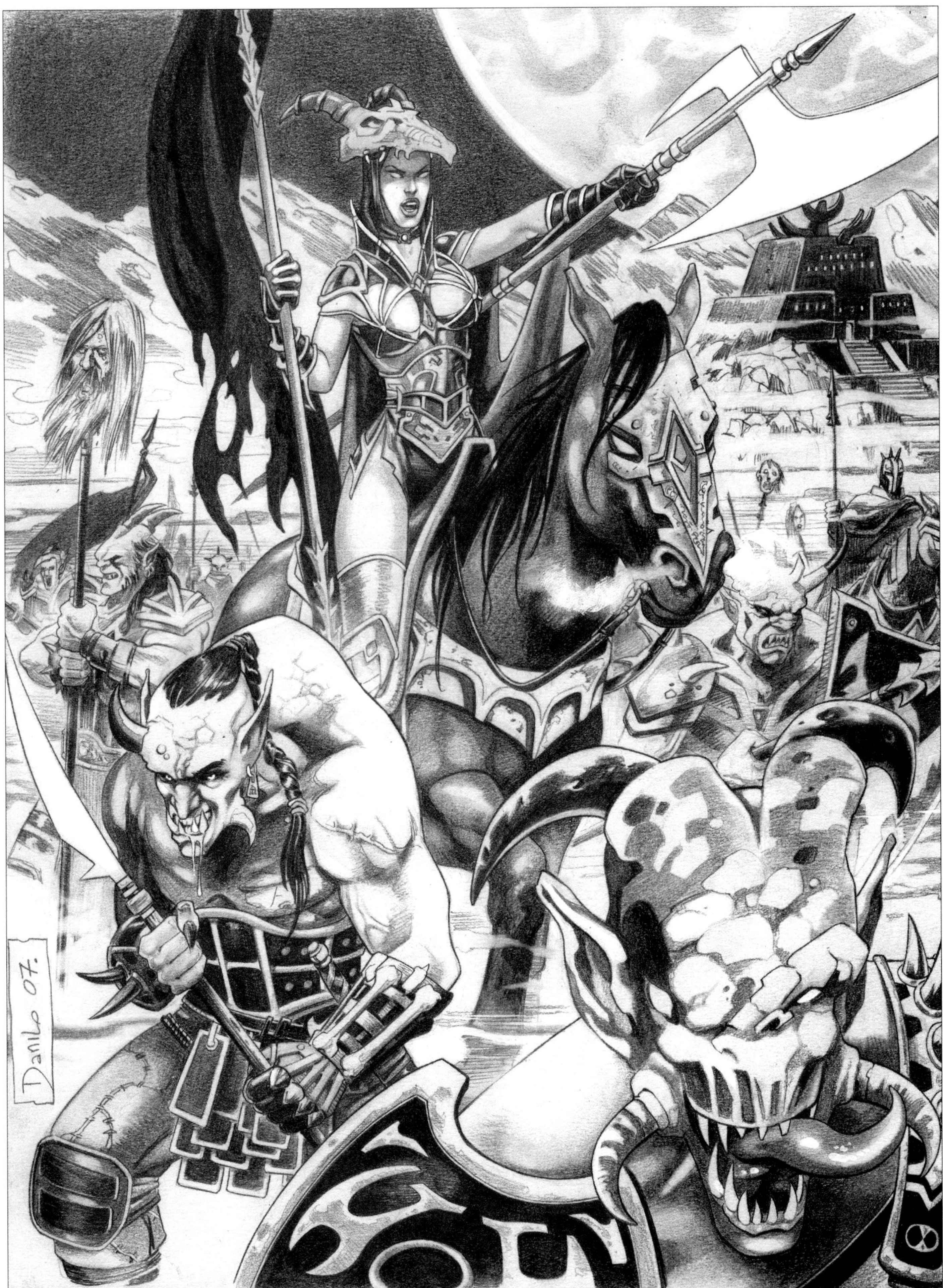

Danilo Guida

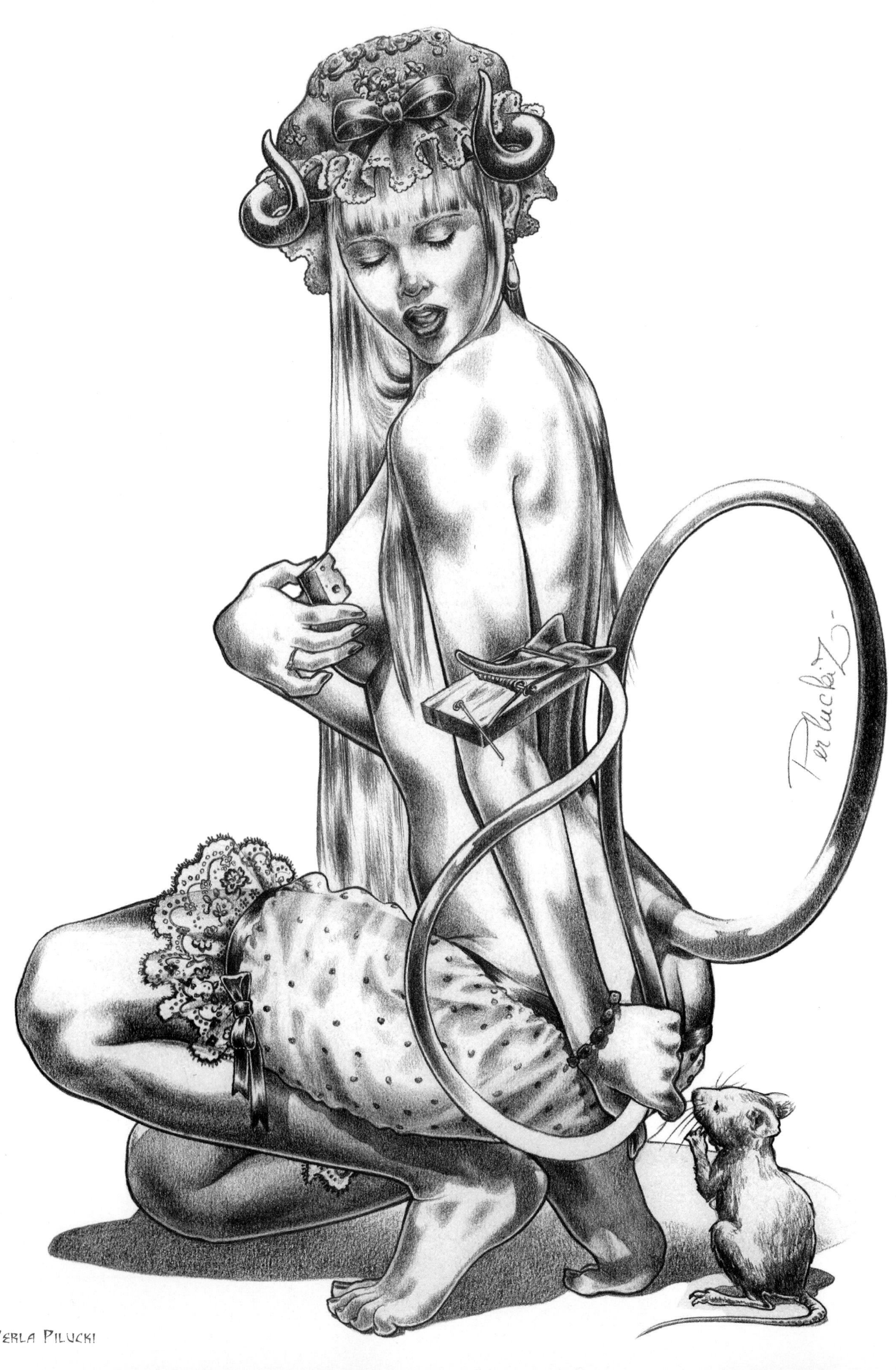

Perla Pilucki

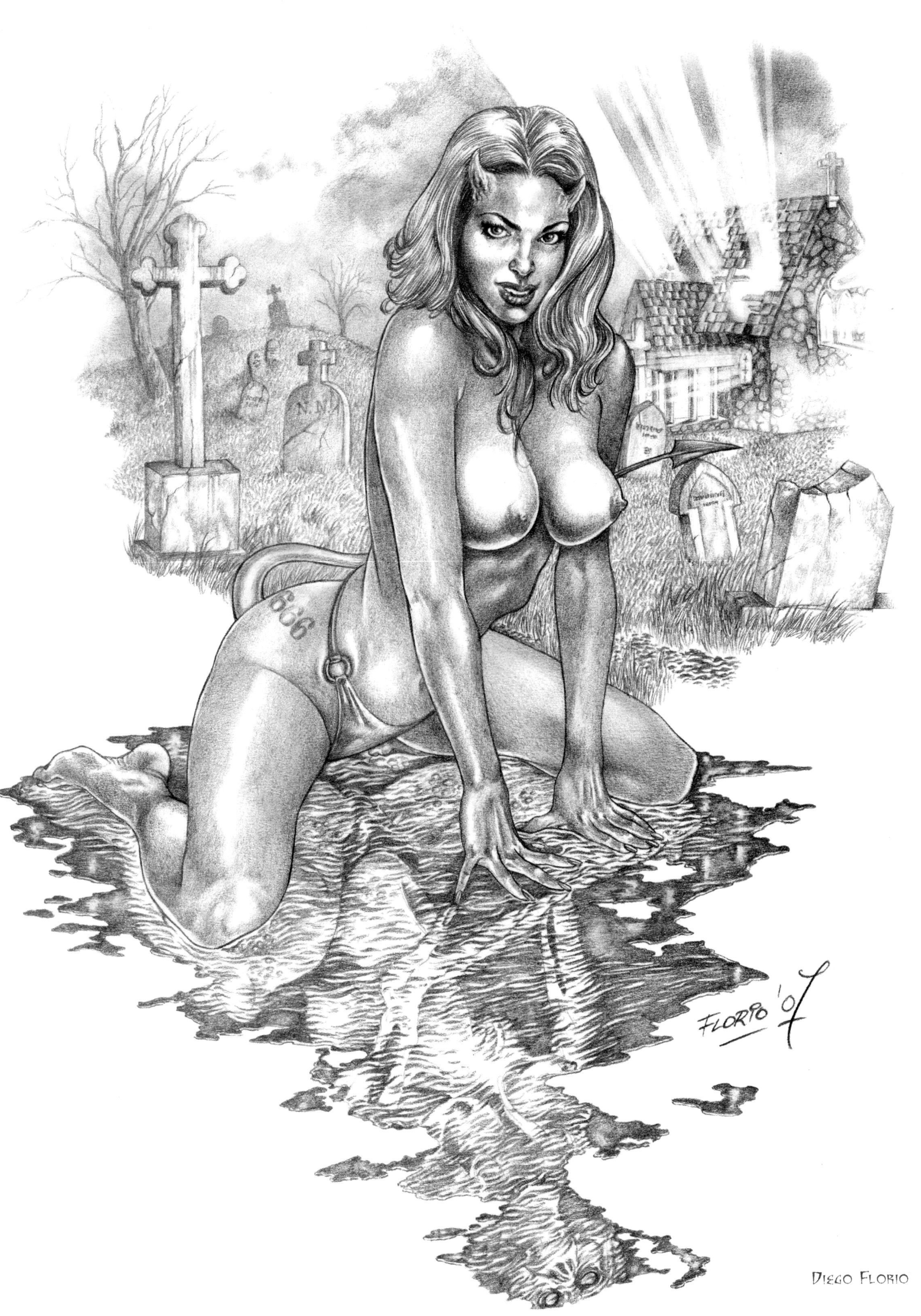
N.N.
FLORIO '07
DIEGO FLORIO

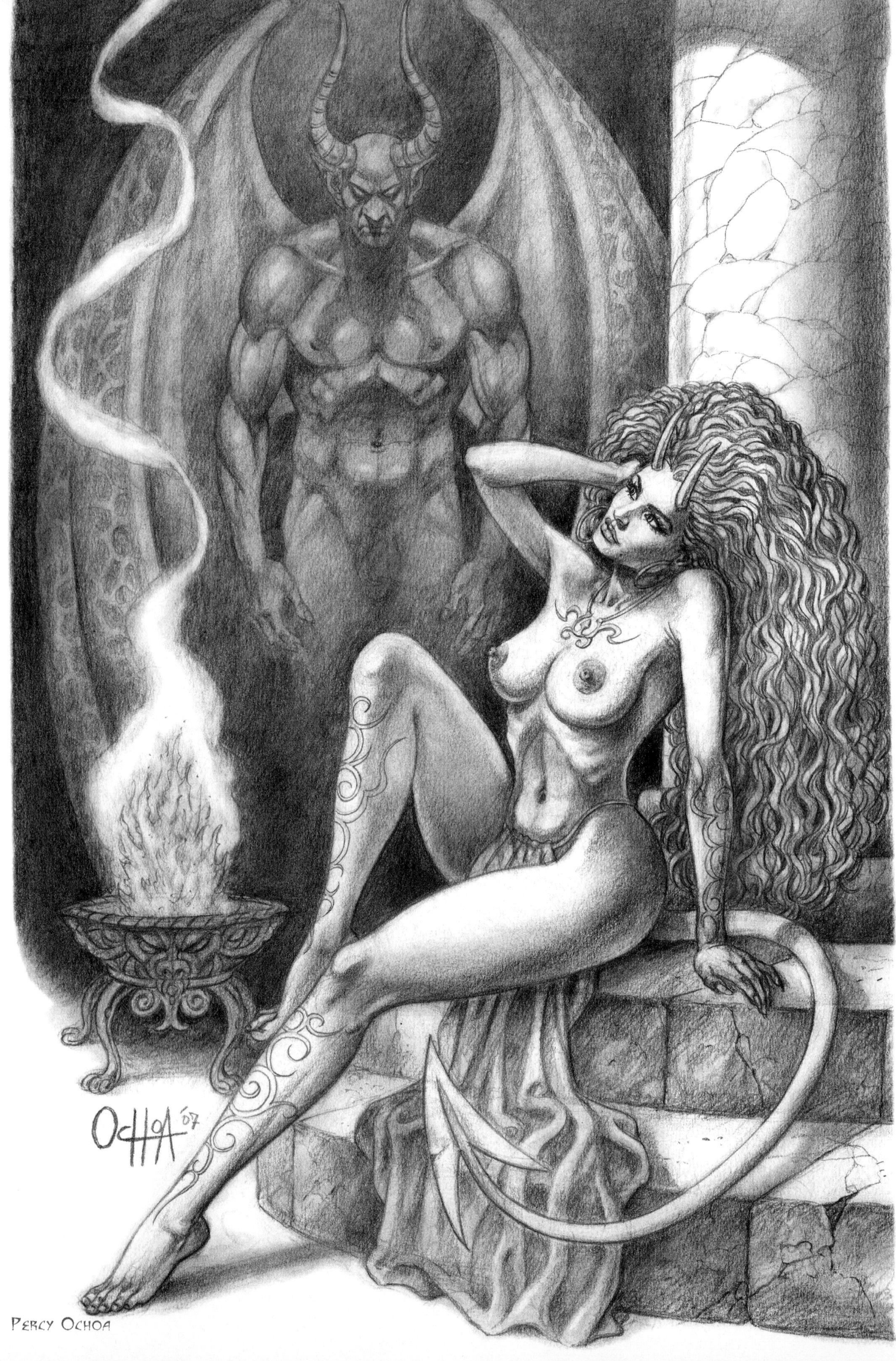

Percy Ochoa

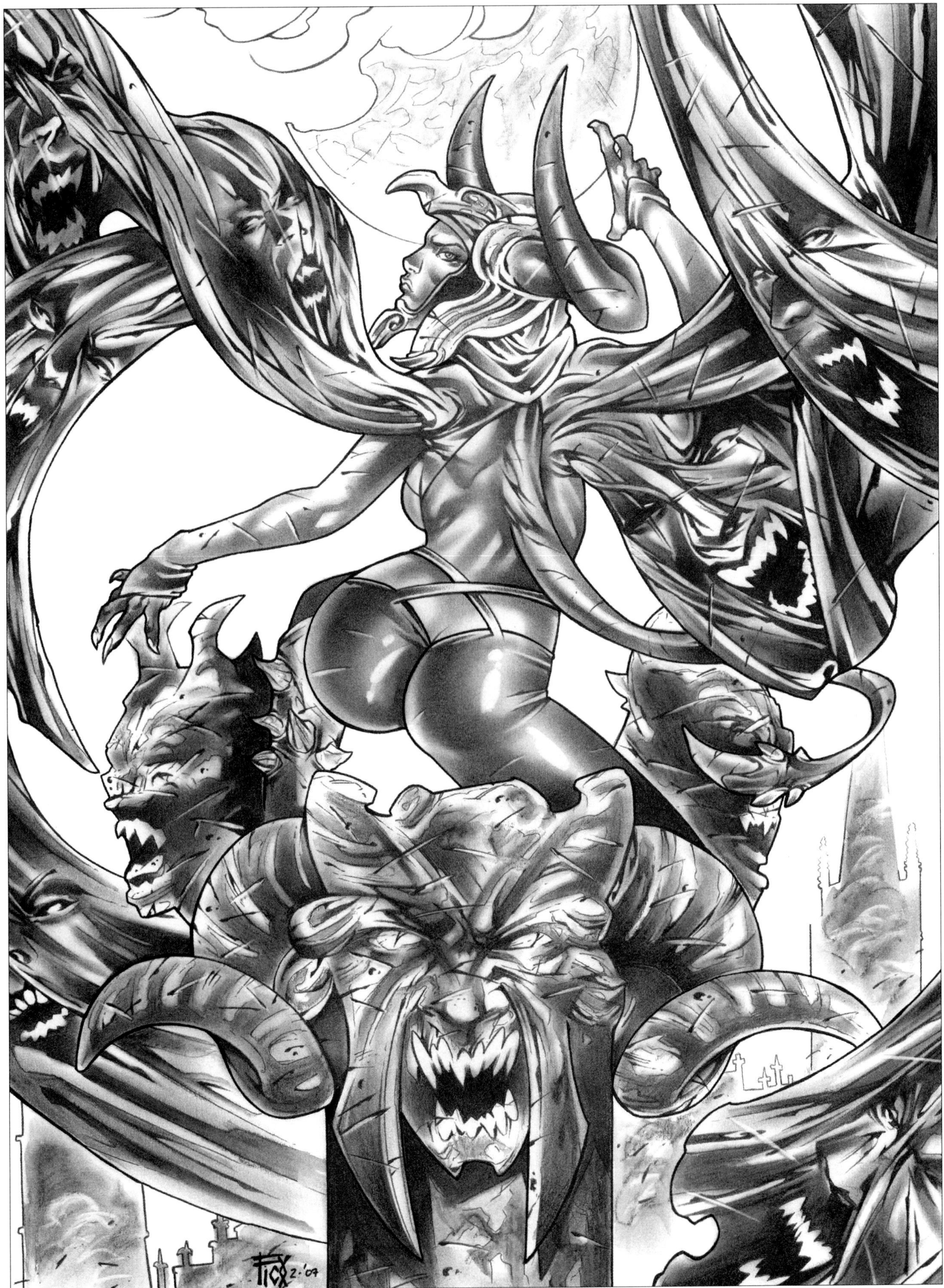

Federico Ossio

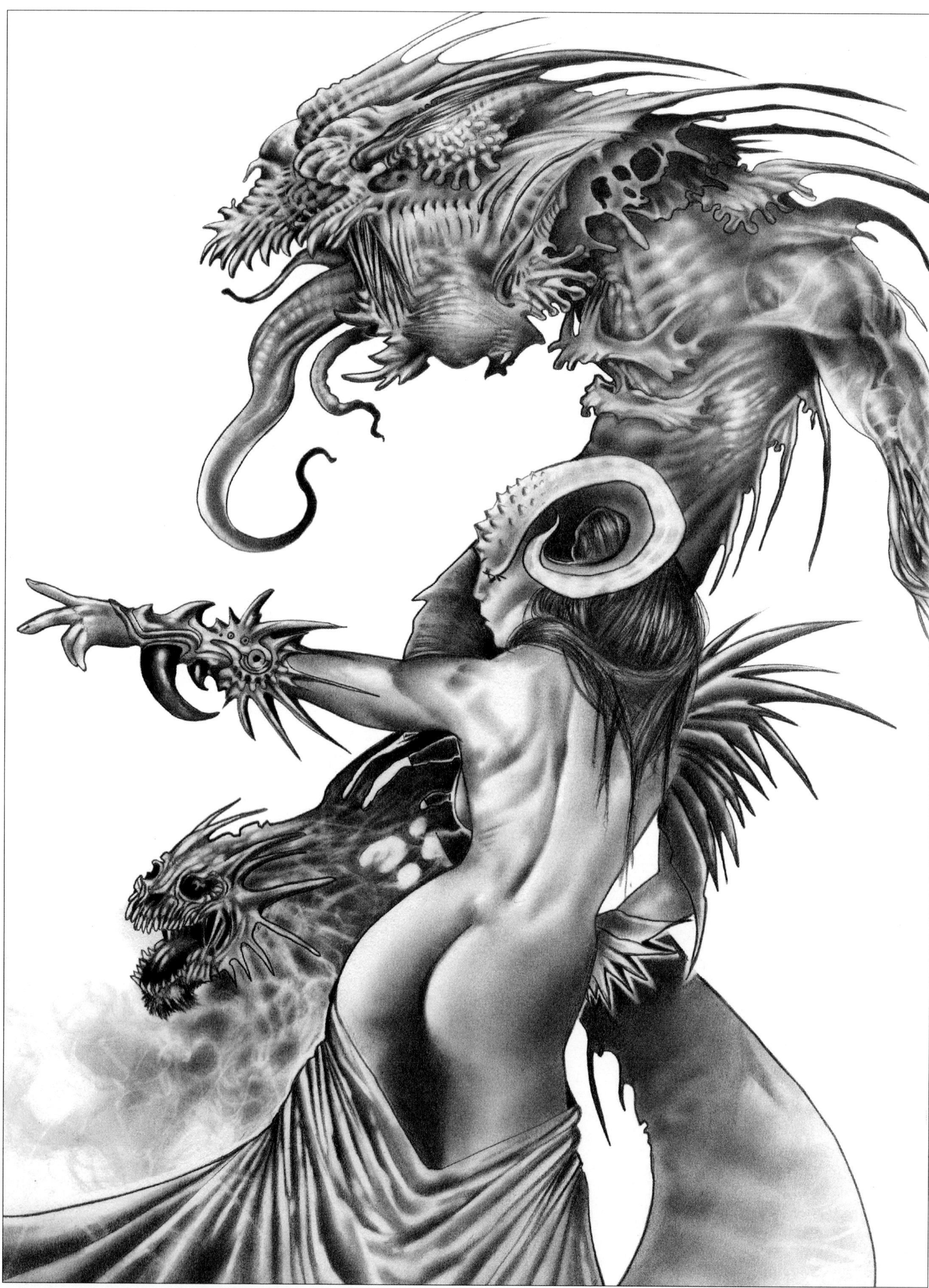

Luis Buci

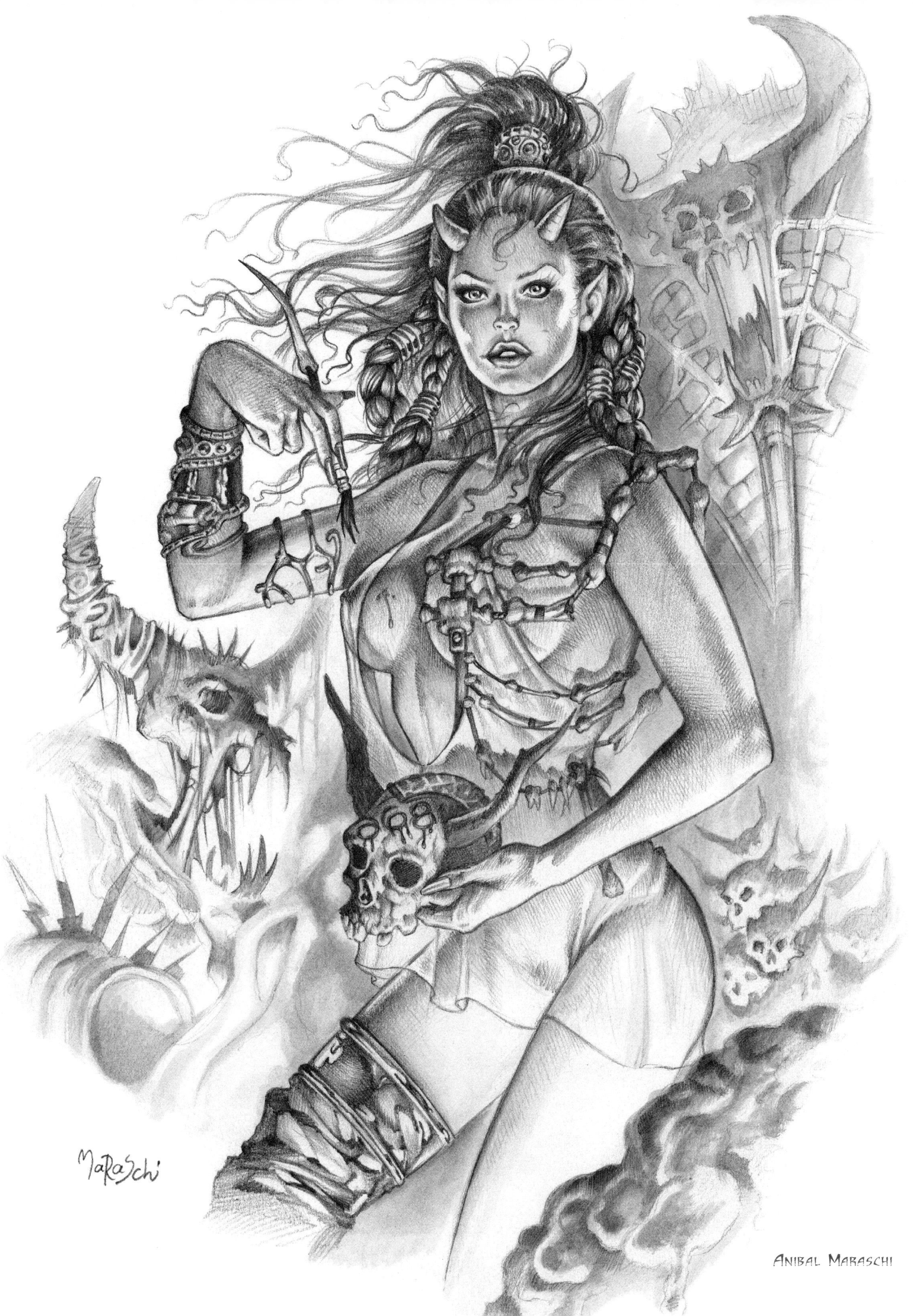

Anibal Maraschi

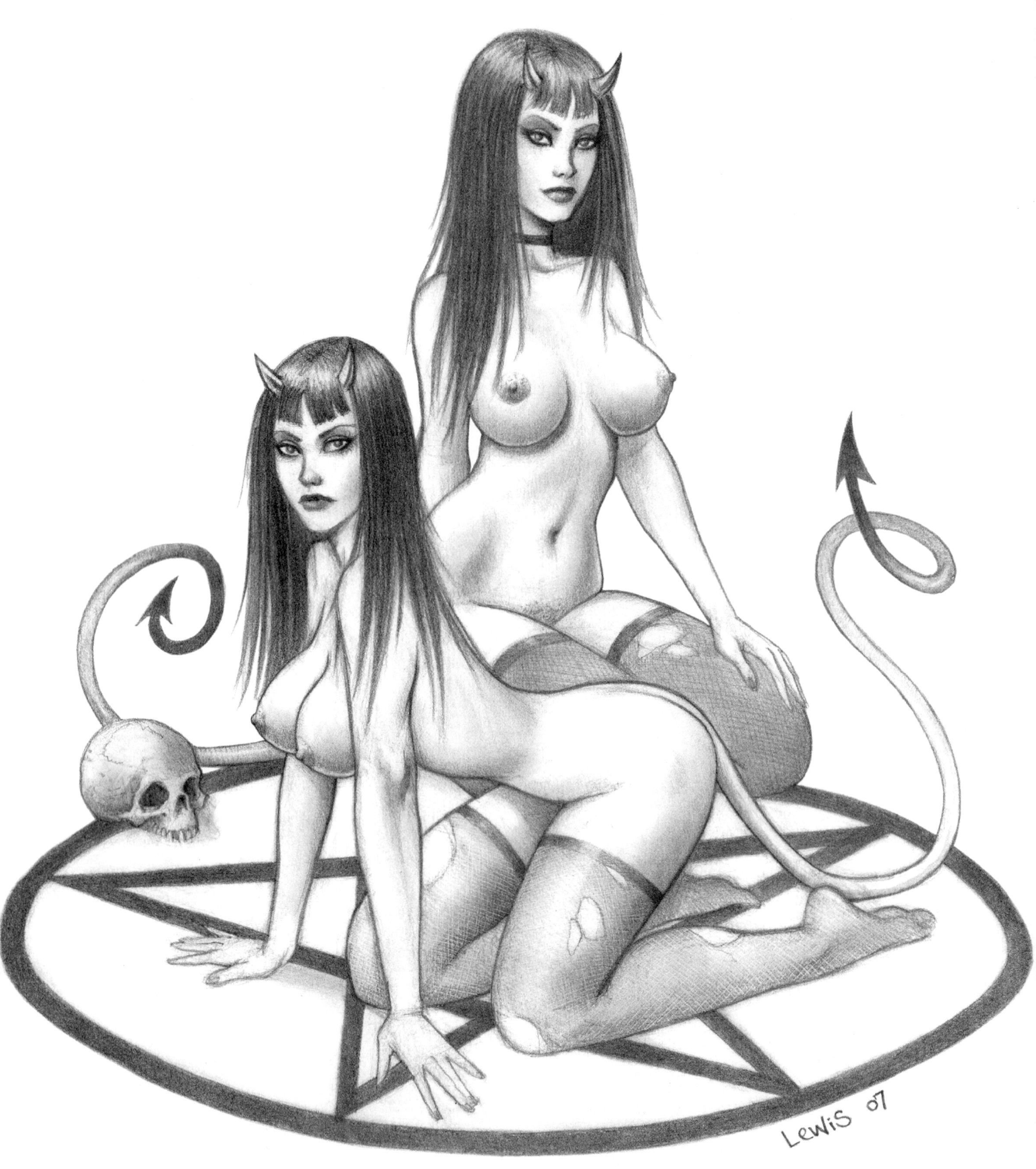

SCOTT LEWIS

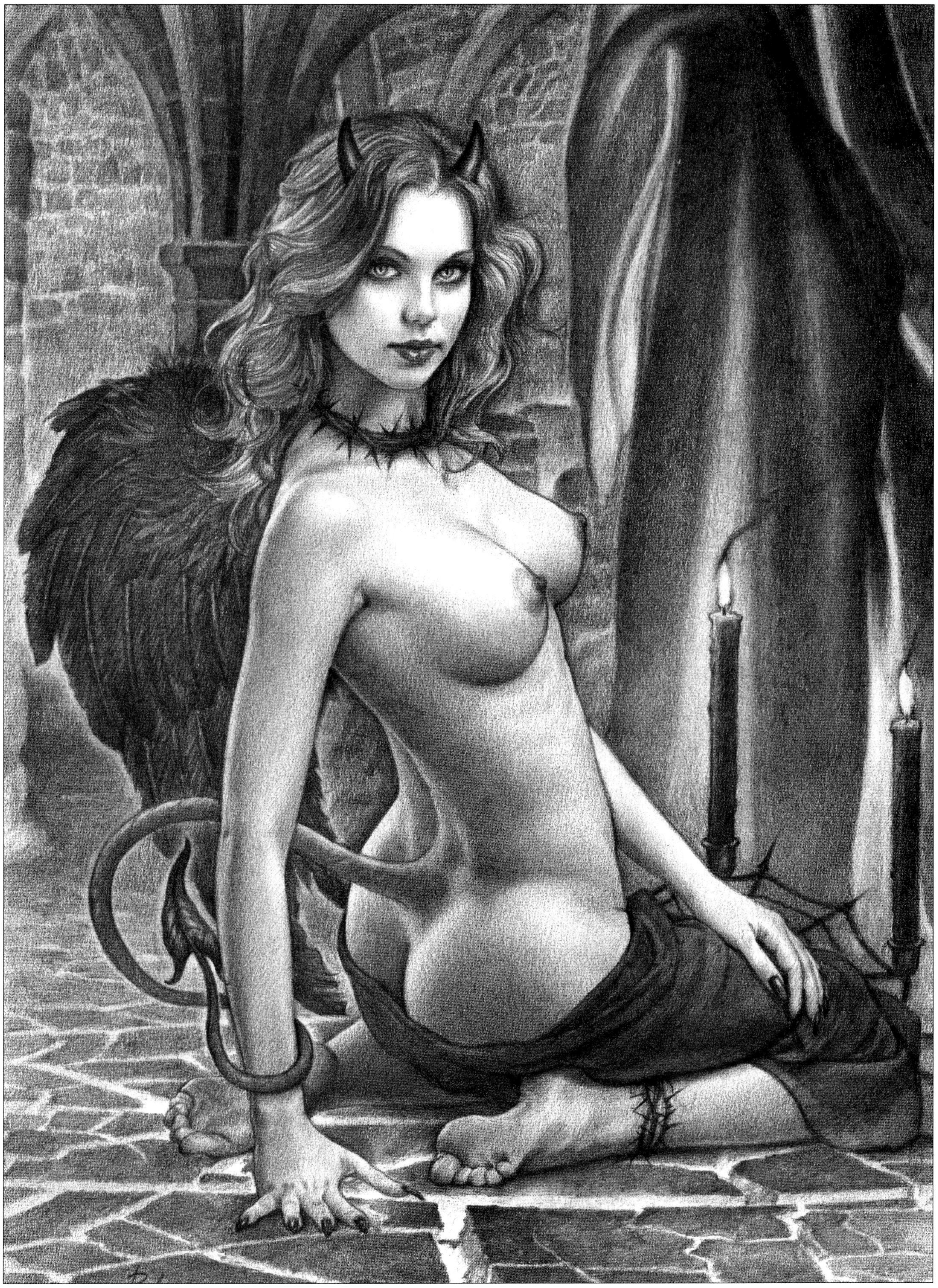

Pelaez

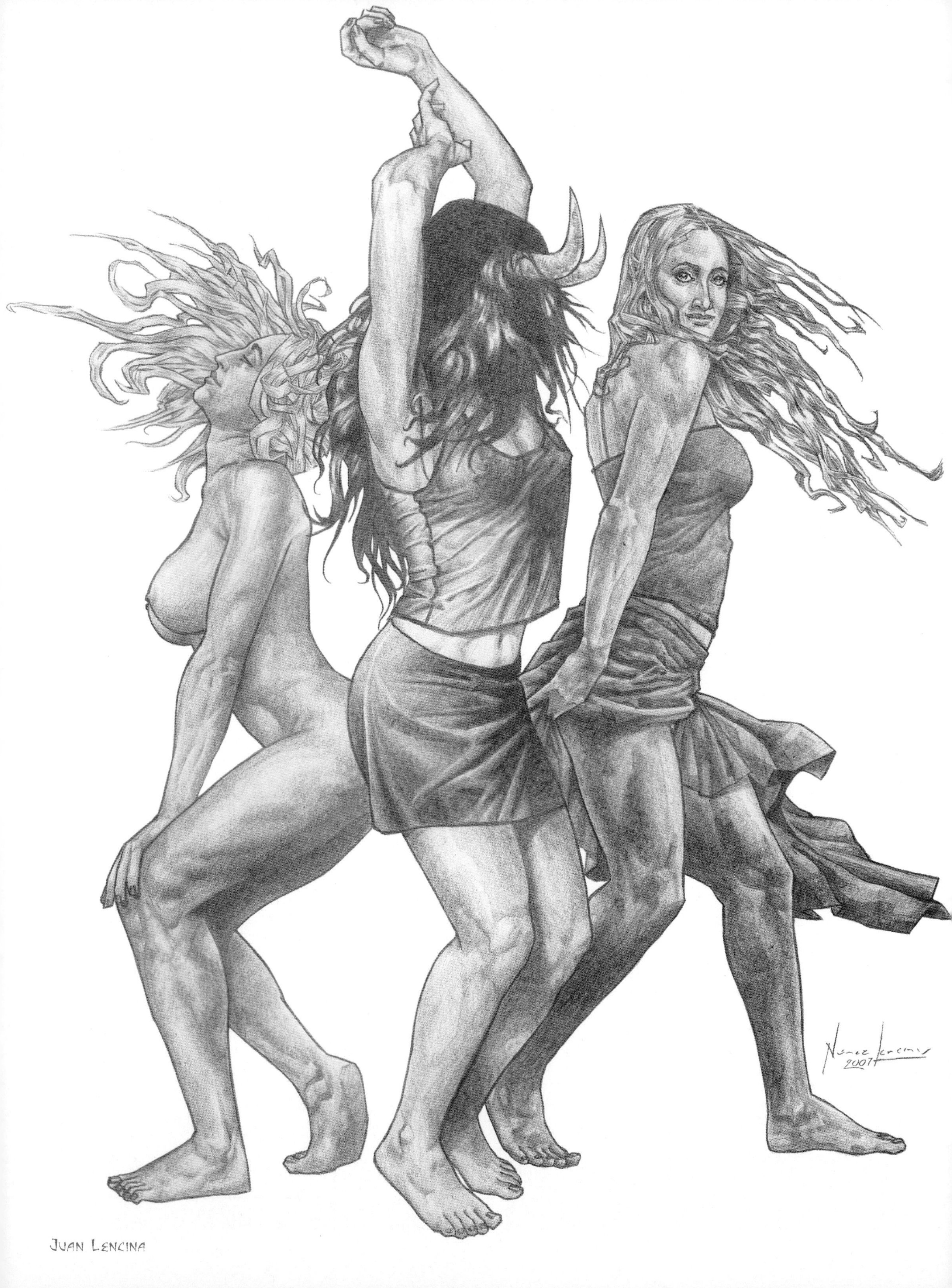

Juan Lencina

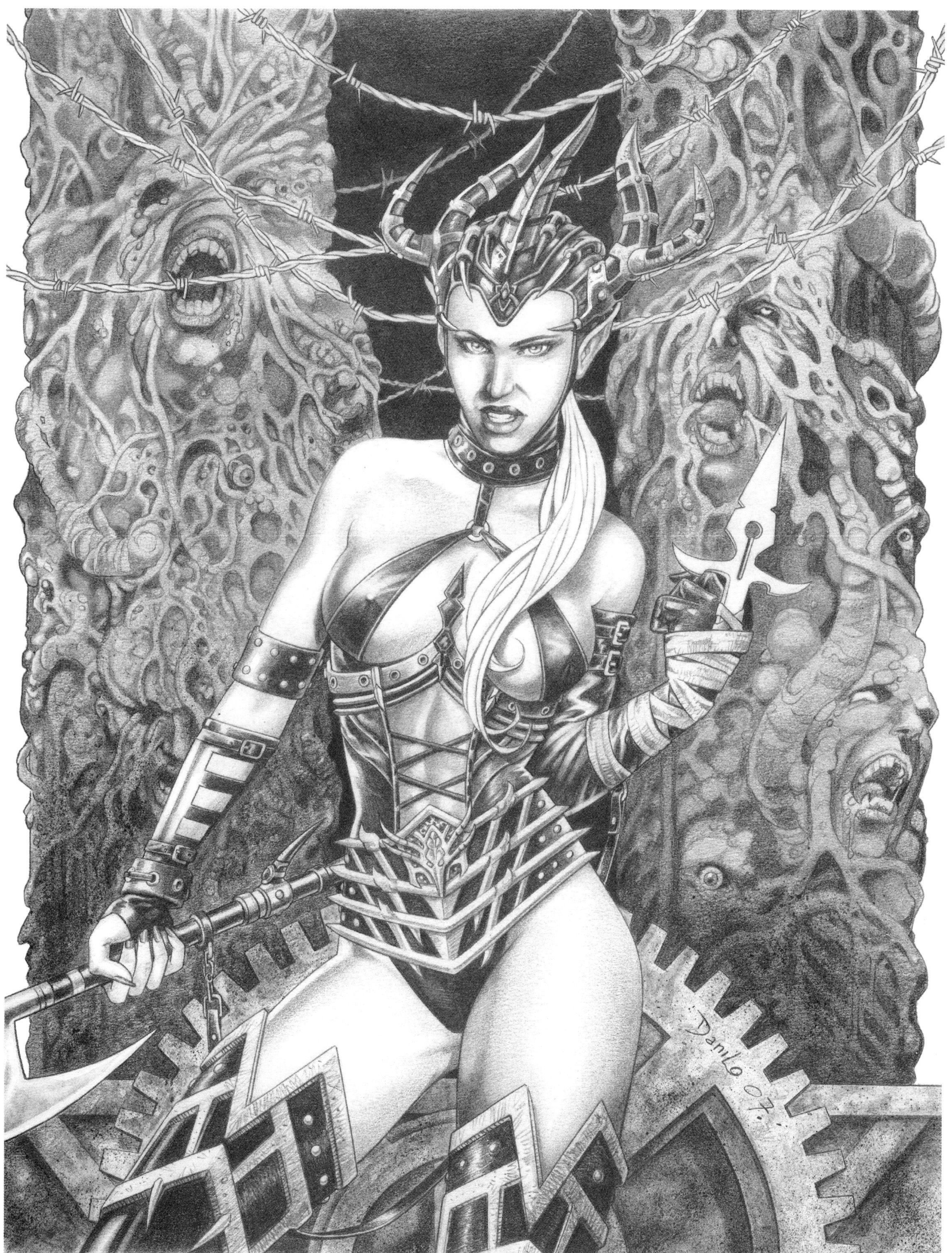

DANILO GUIDA

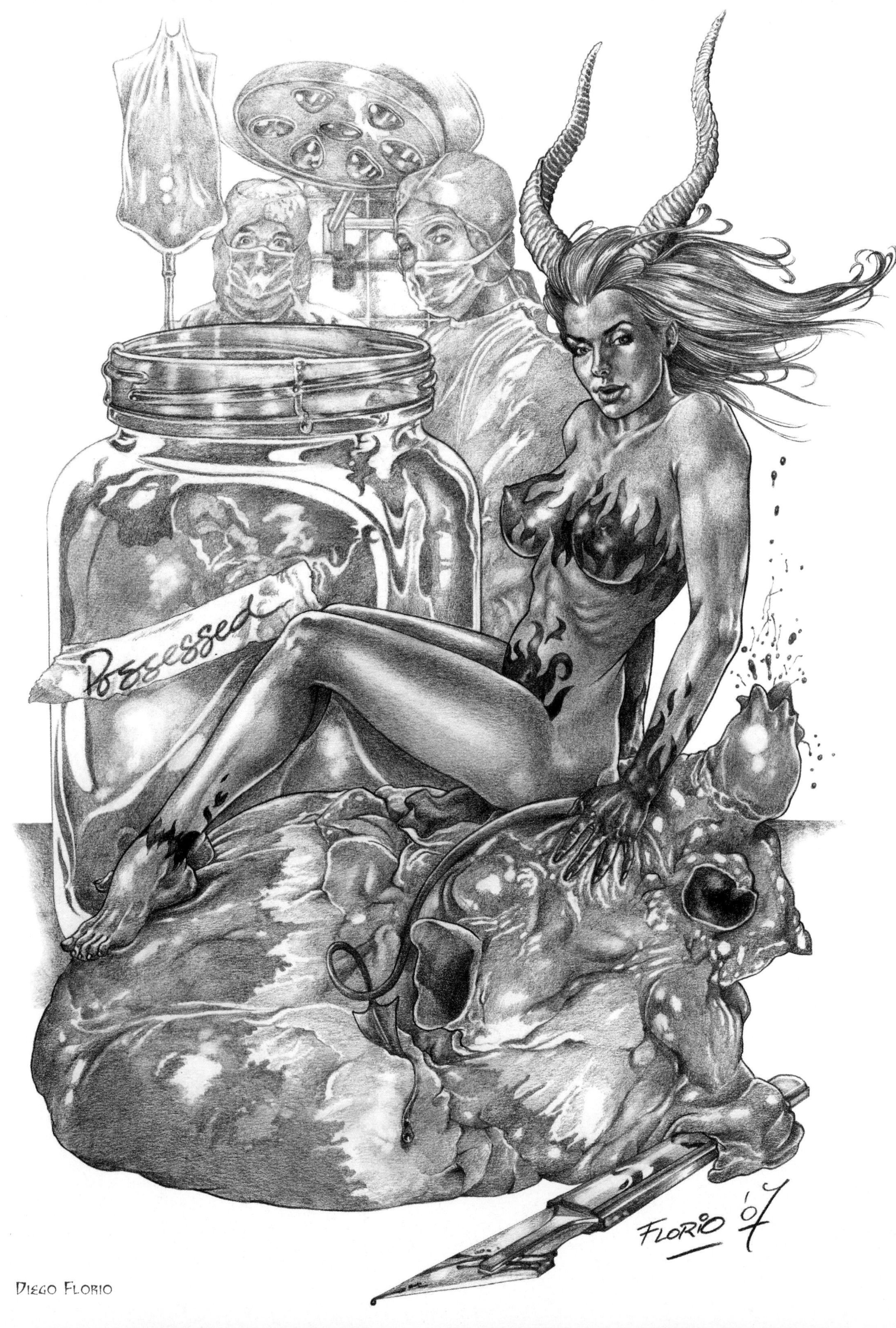

Diego Florio

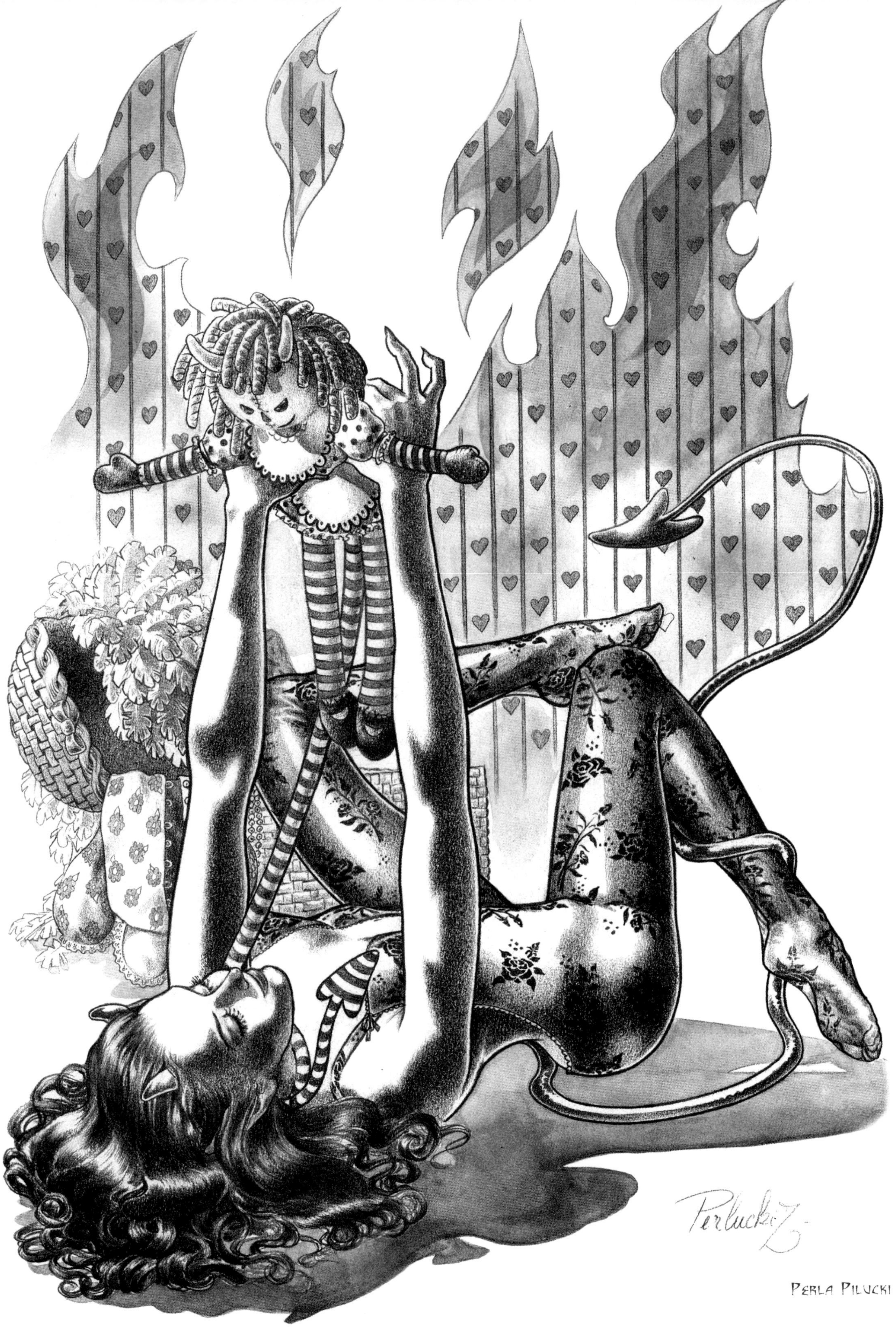

Perla Pilucki

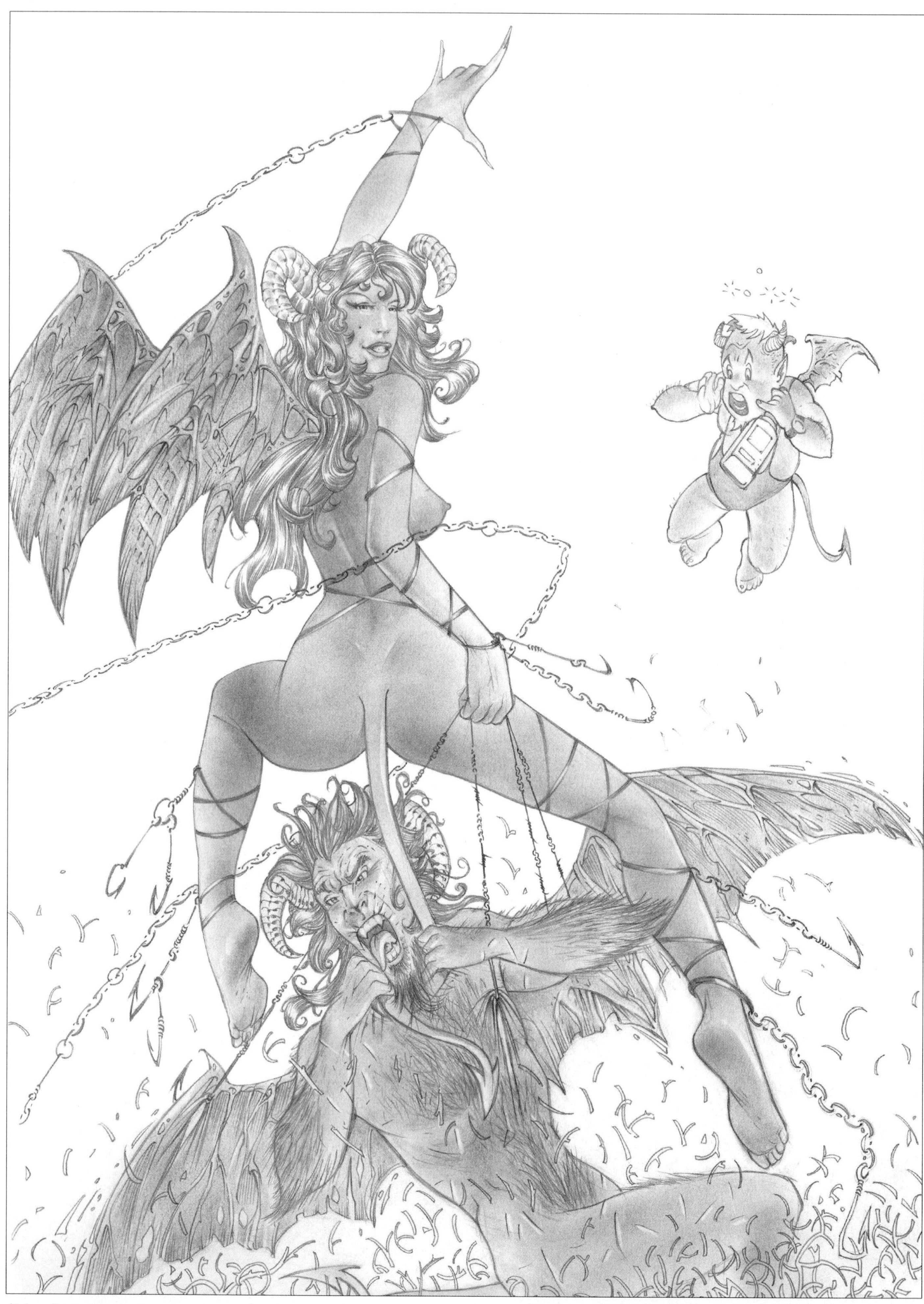

J.L. Czerniawski

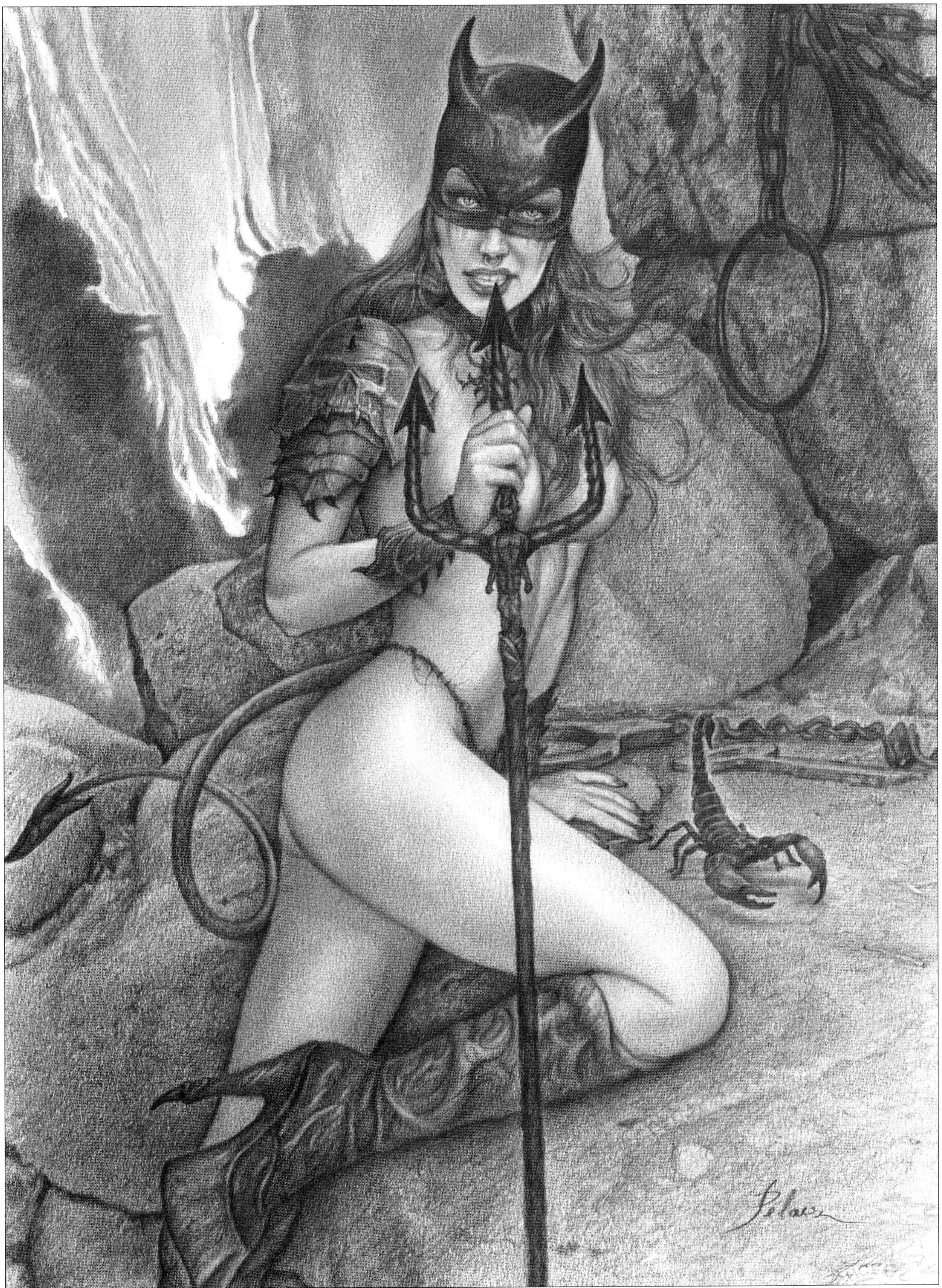

Pelaez

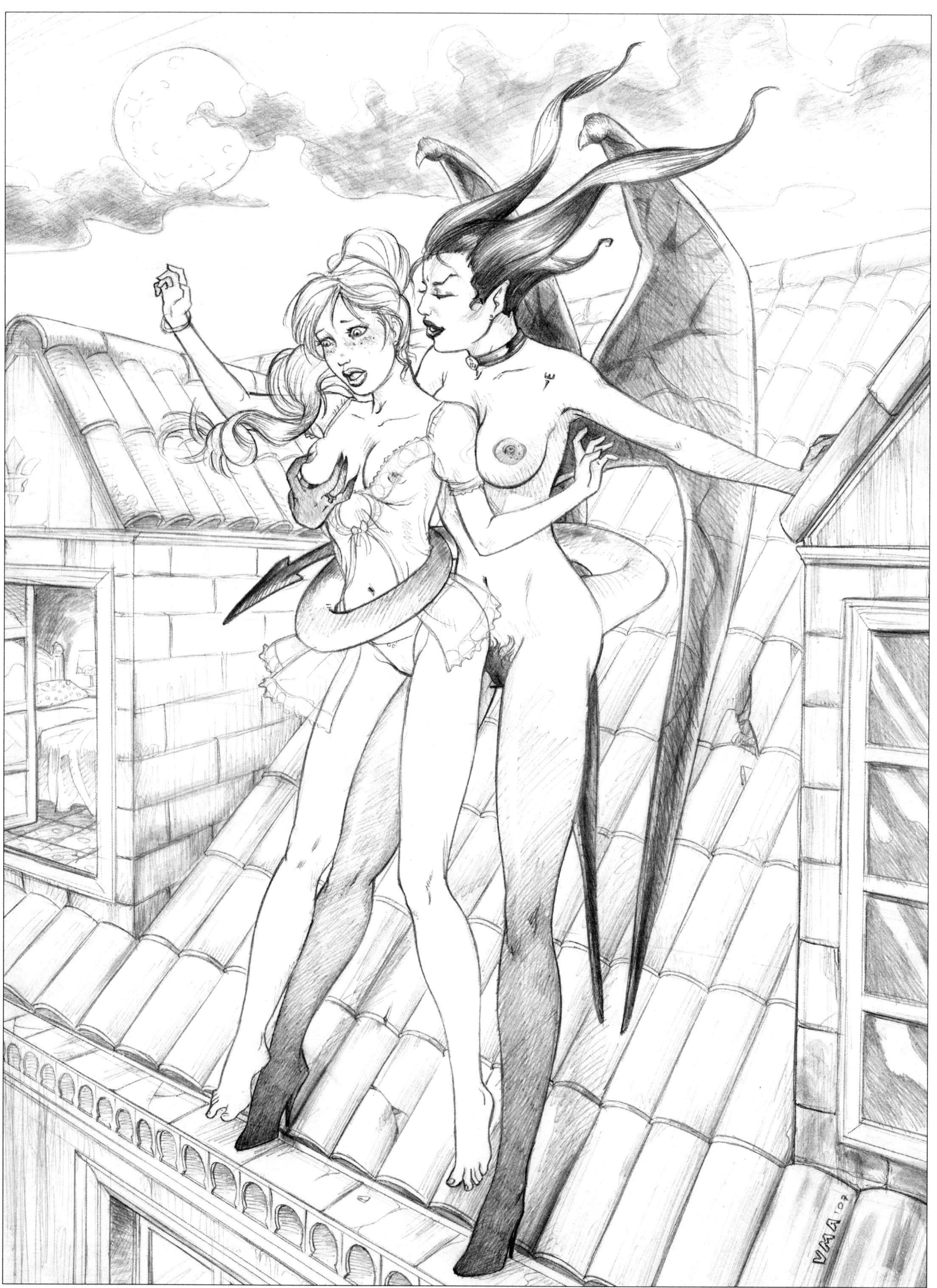

Victor Ahmed

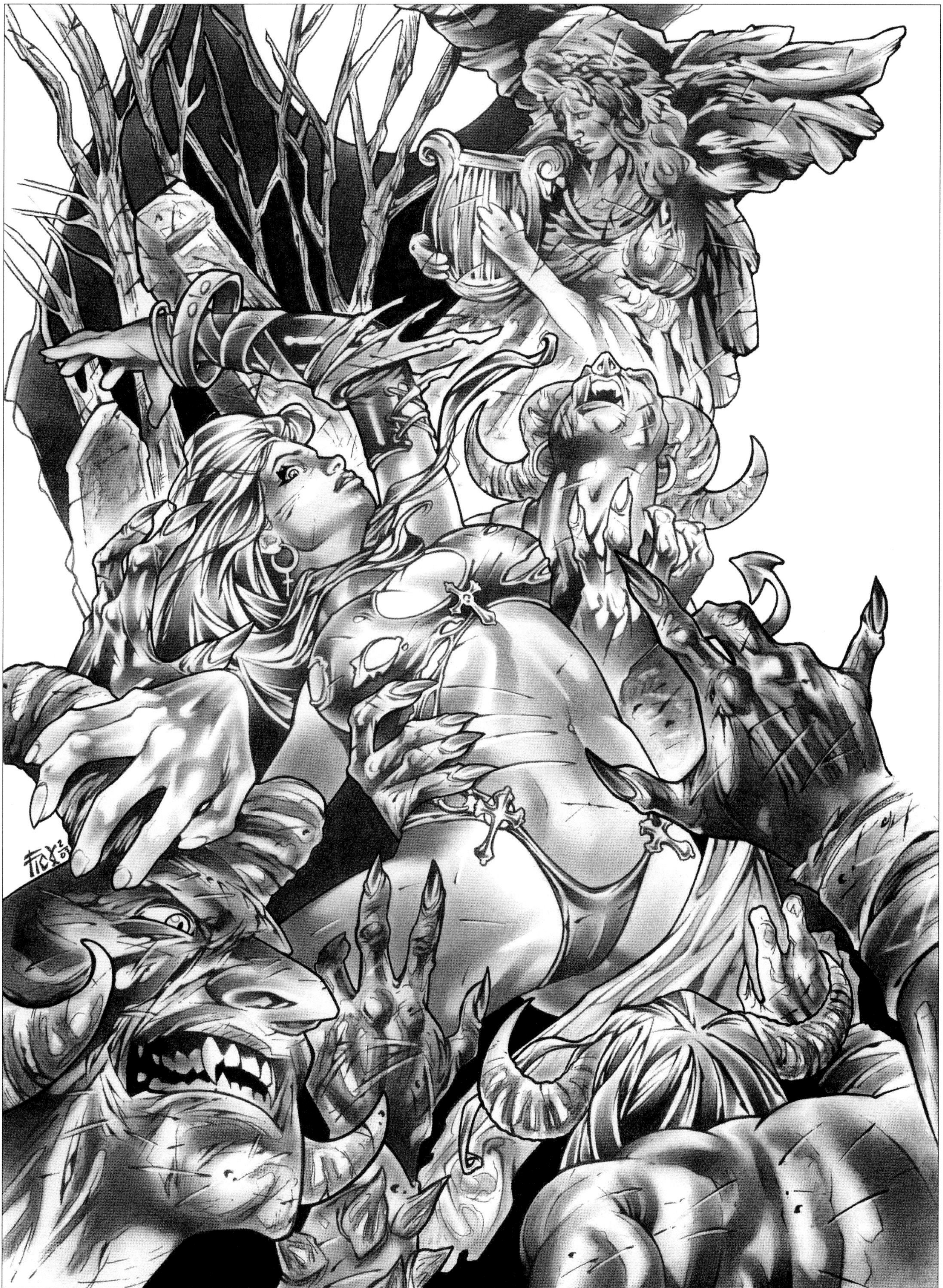

Federico Ossio

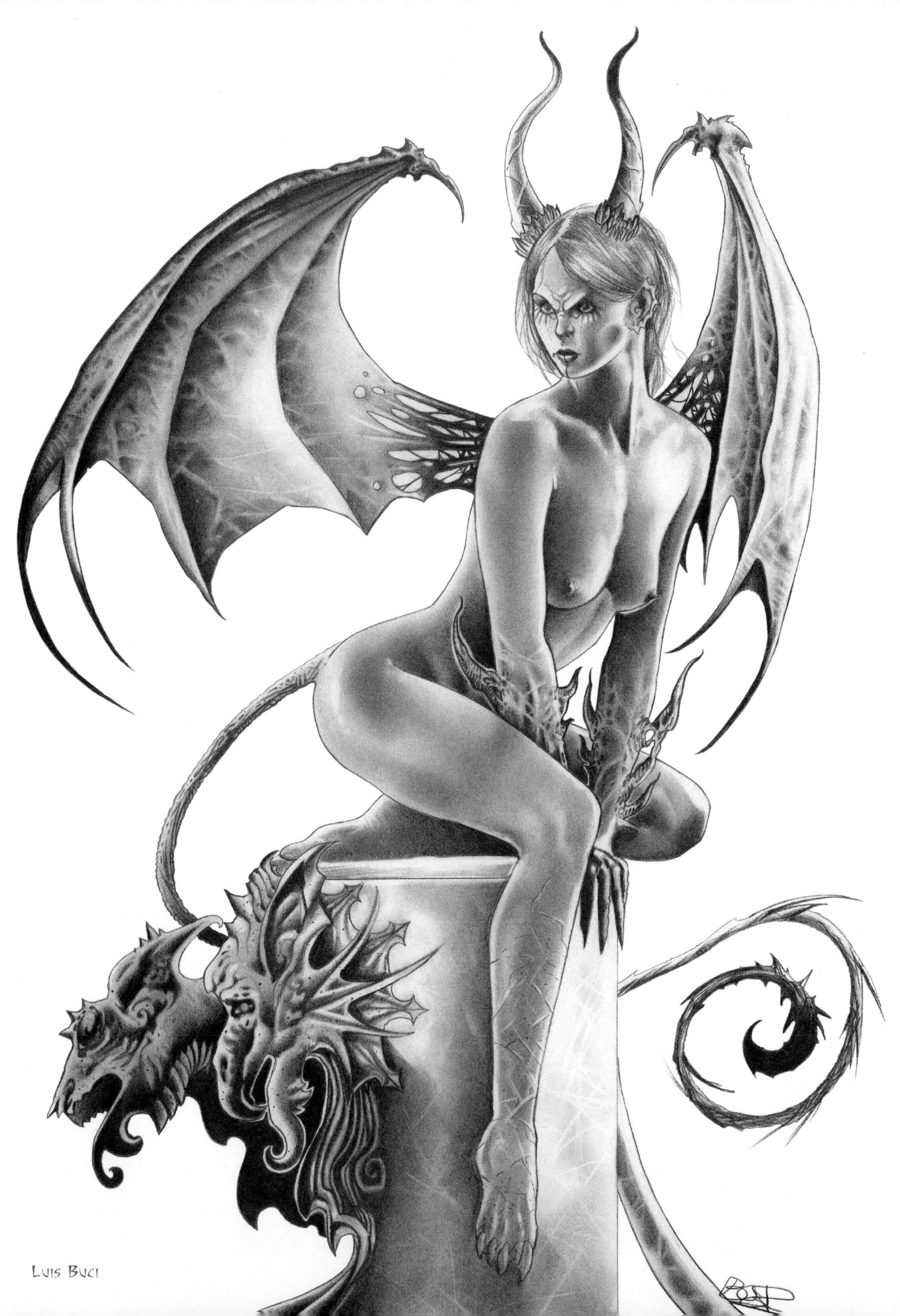

Luis Buci

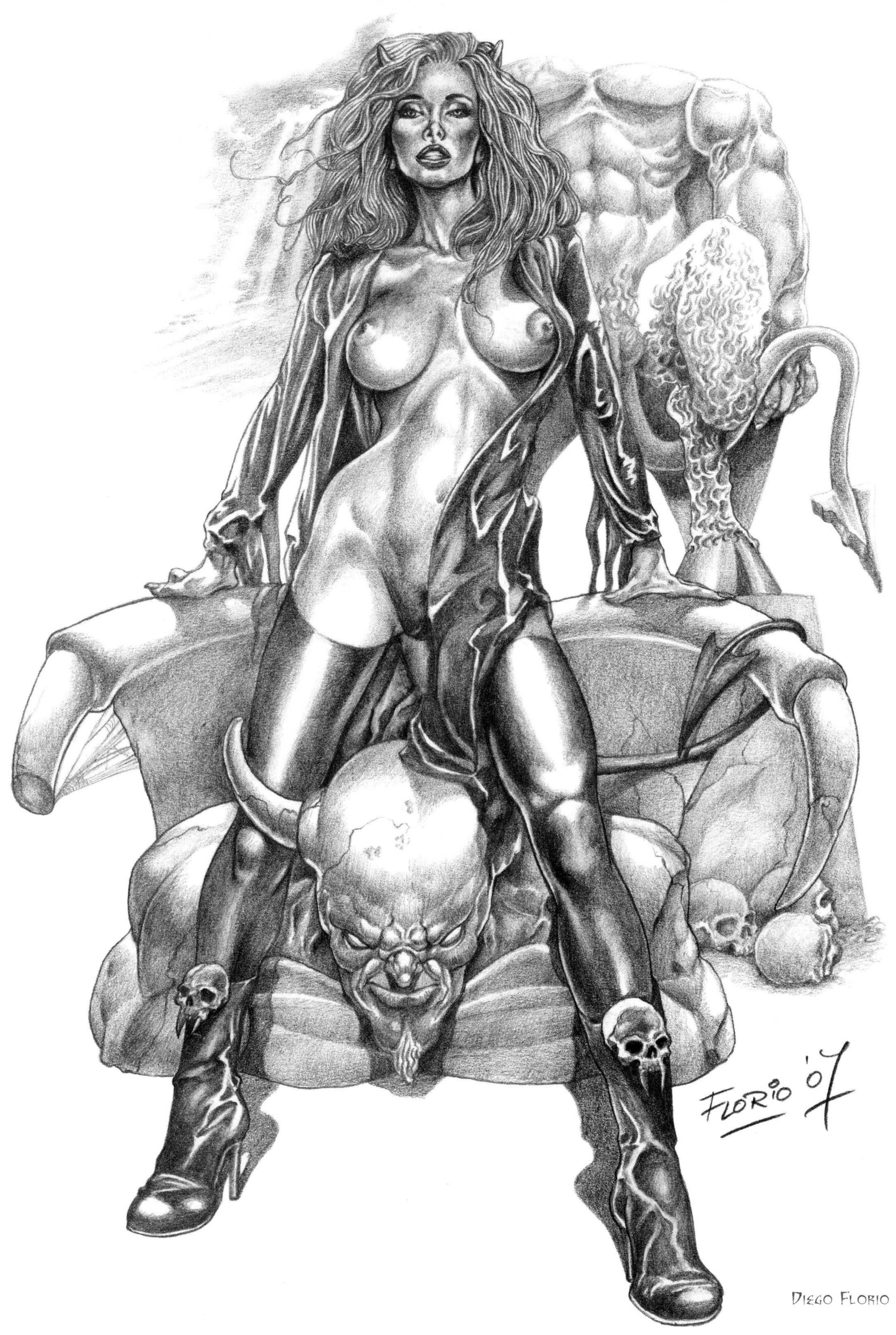

DIEGO FLORIO

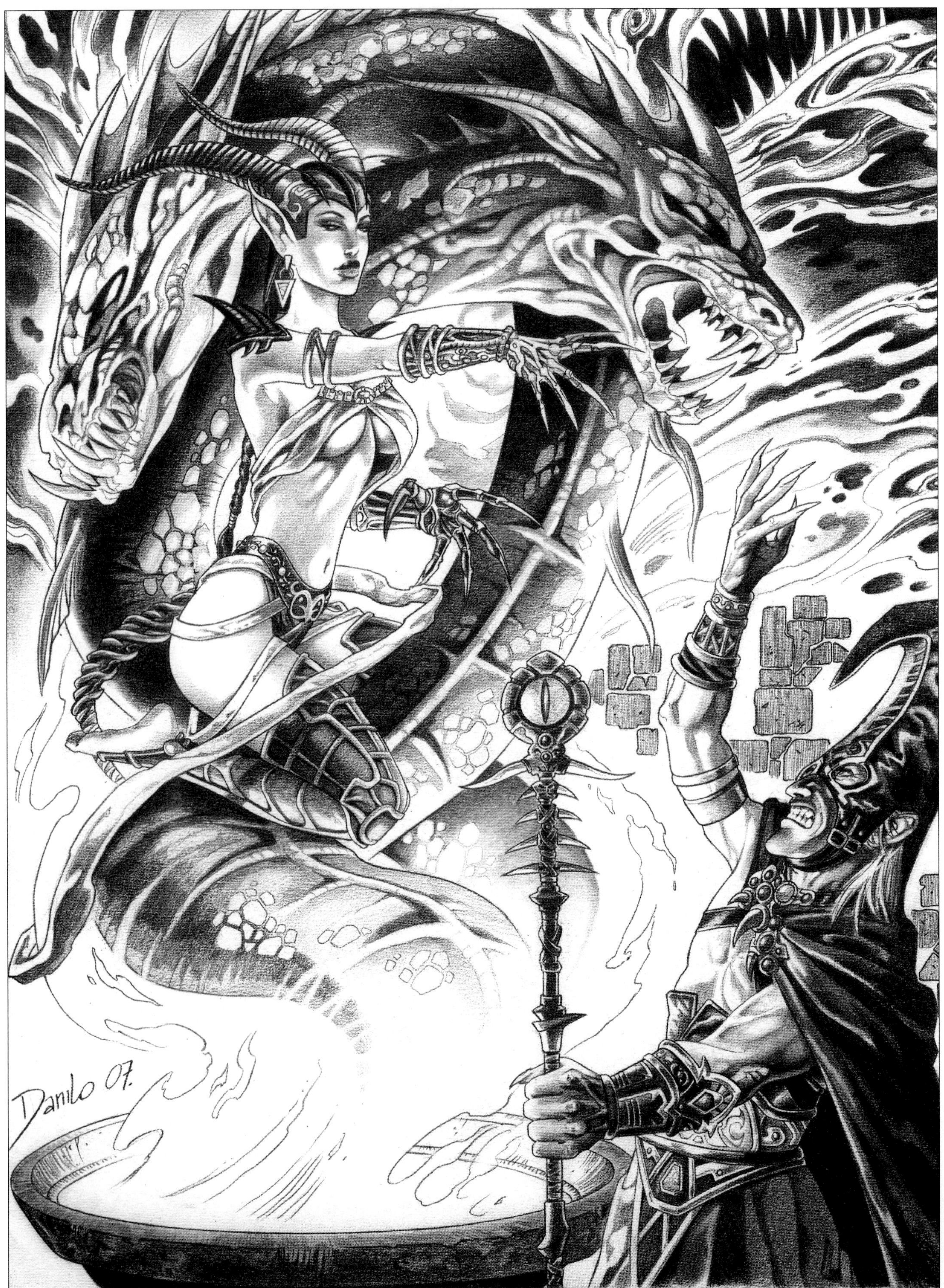

DANILO GUIDA

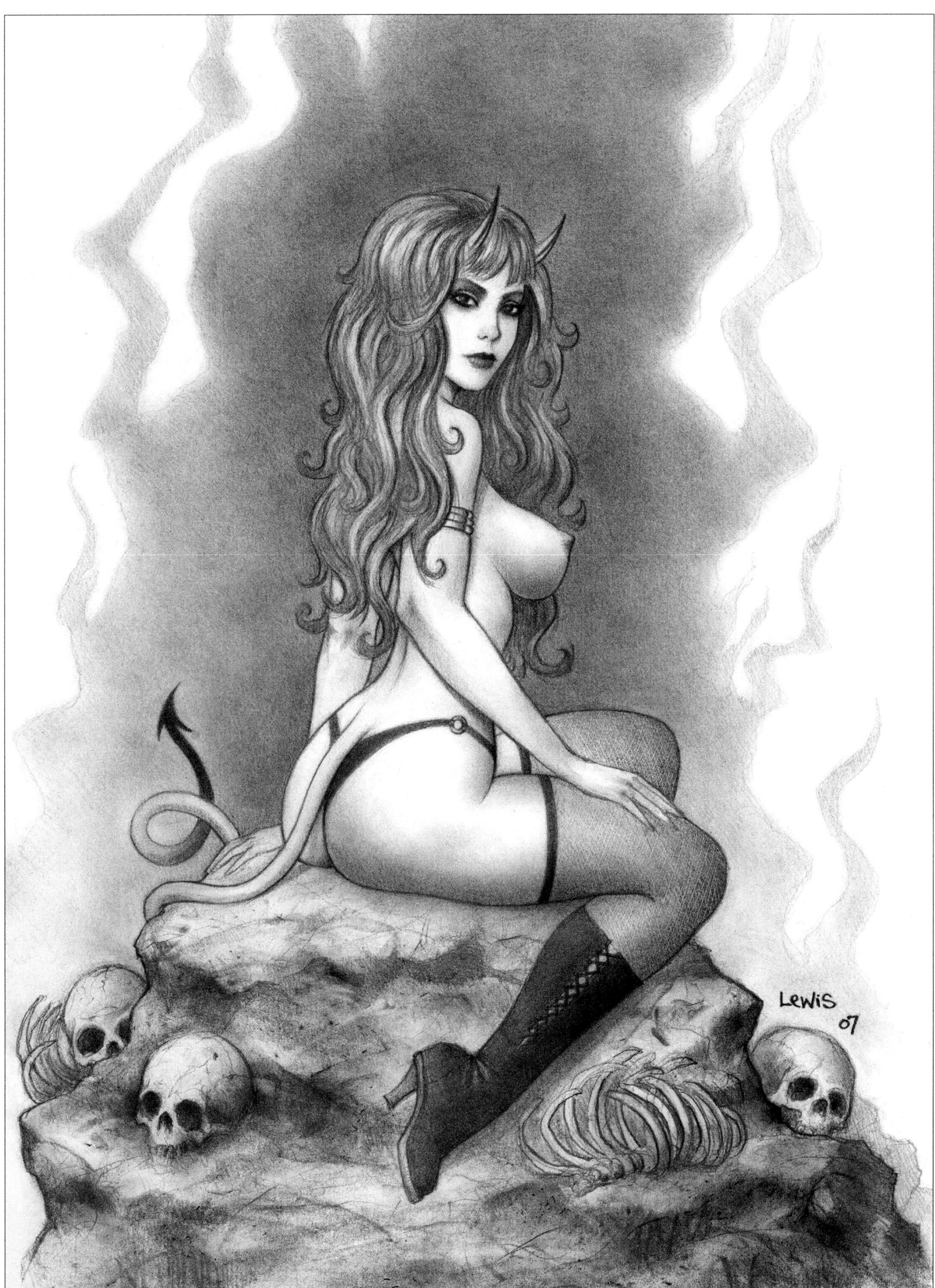

Scott Lewis

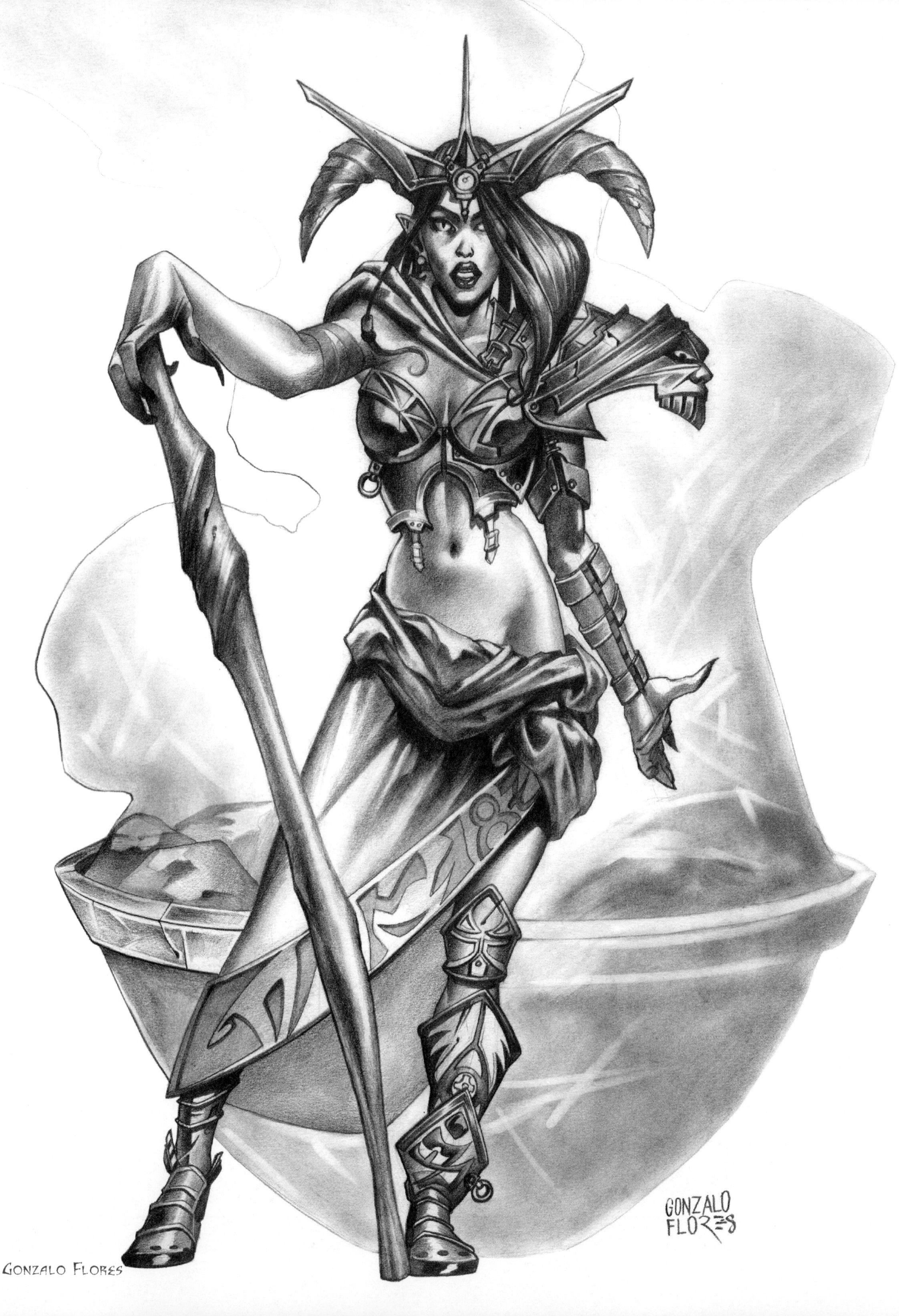

GONZALO FLORES

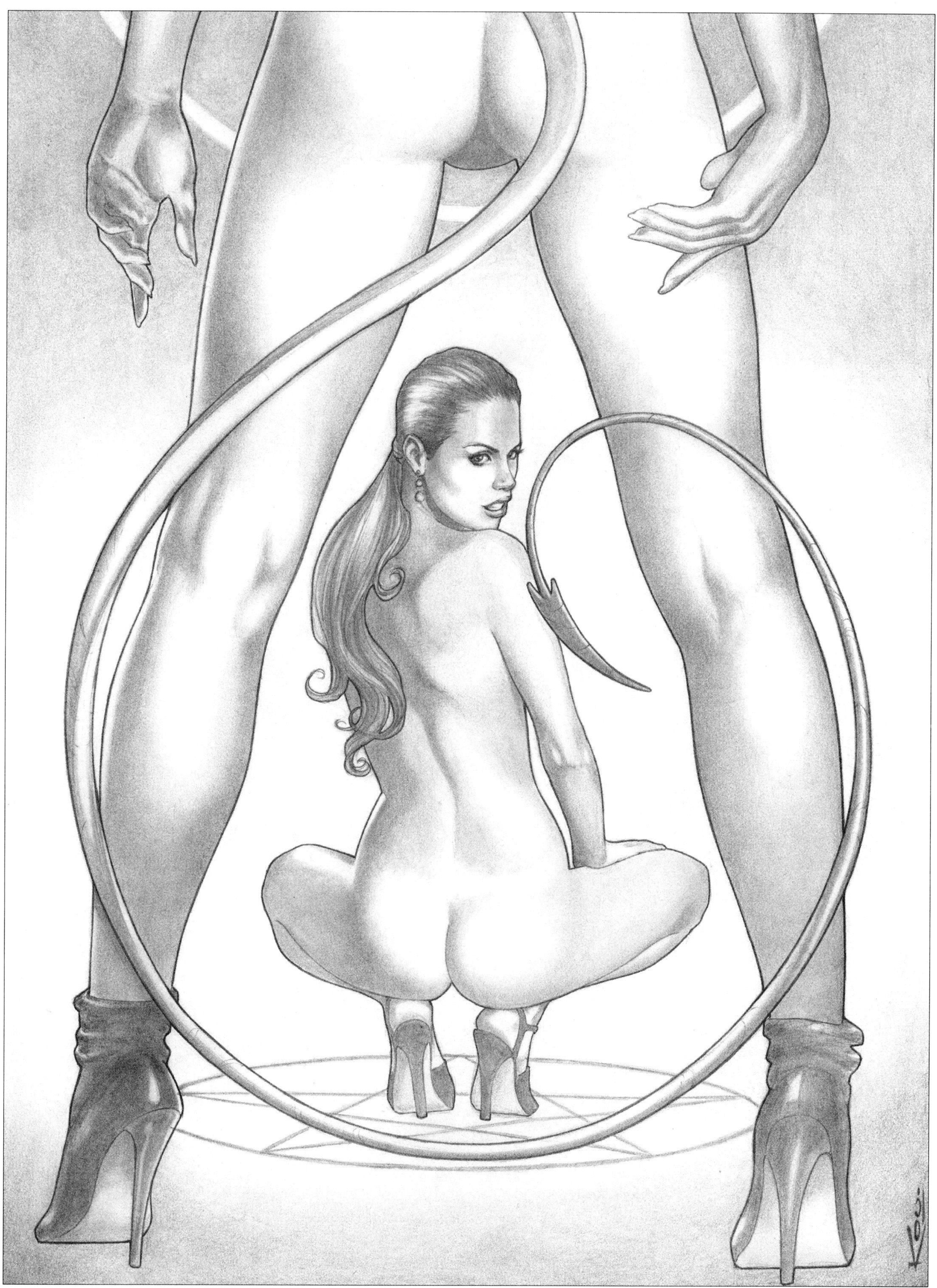

Pablo Kousovitis

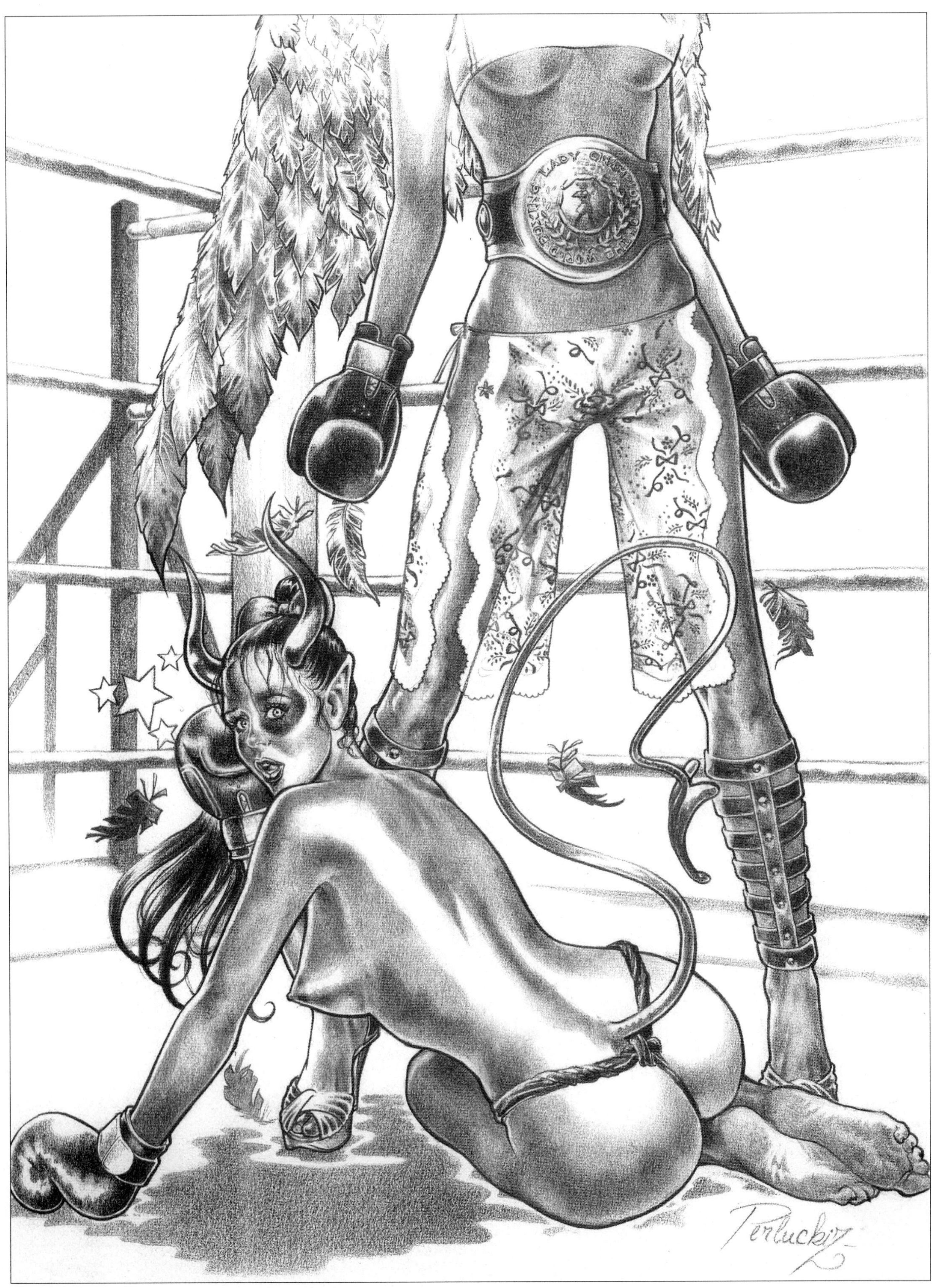

Perla Pilucki

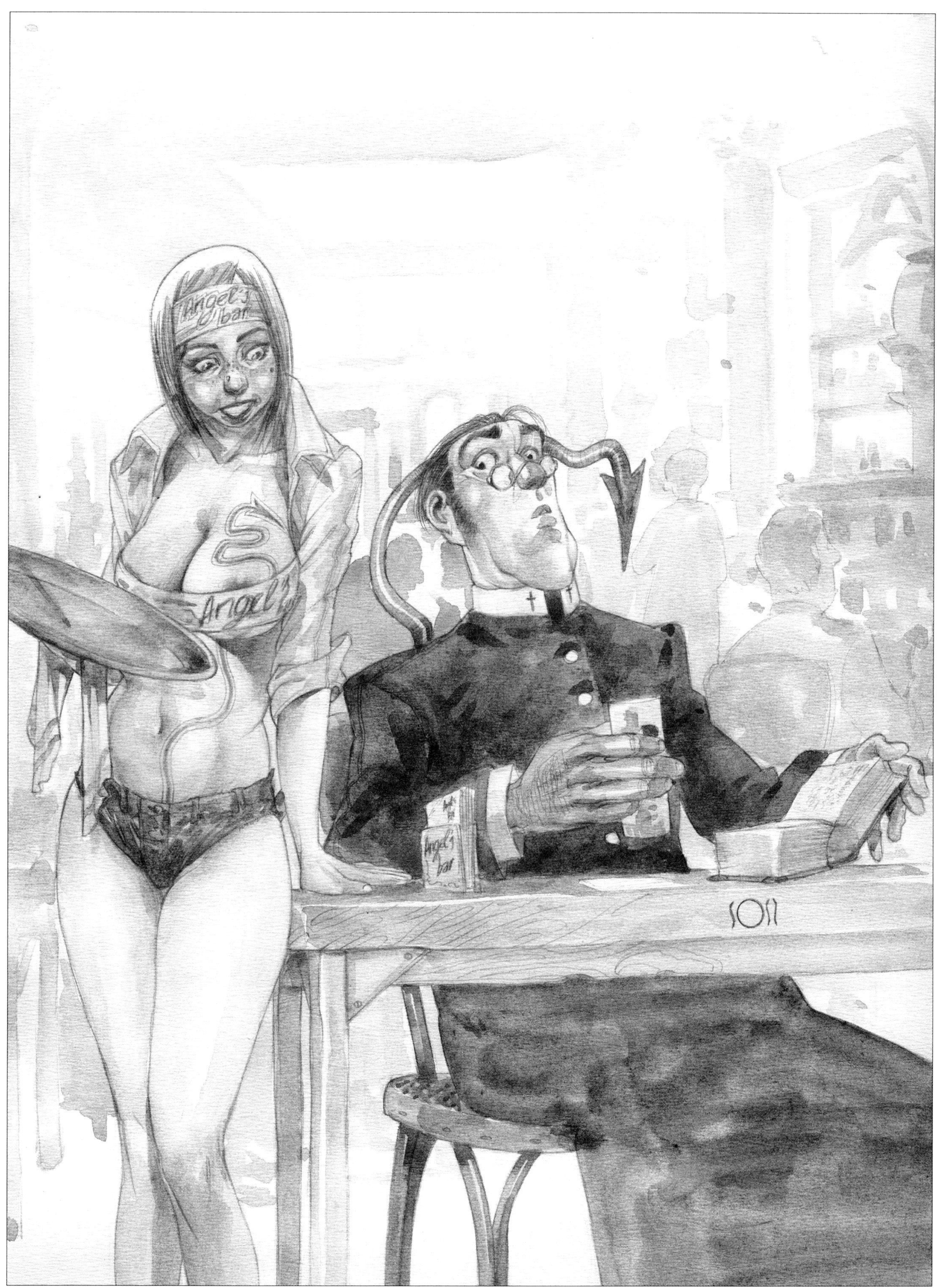

Marcelo Sosa

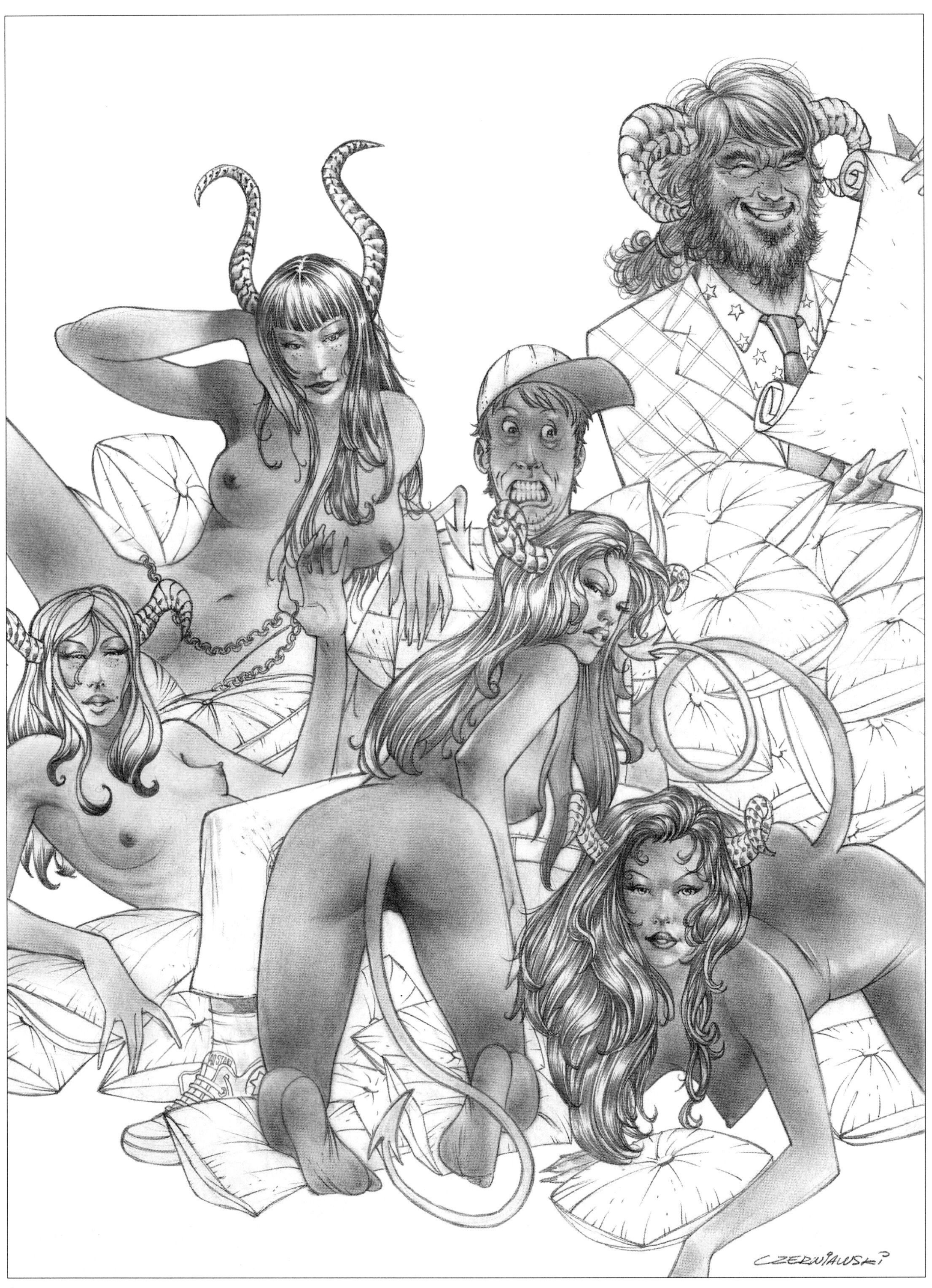

J.L. CZERNIAWSKI

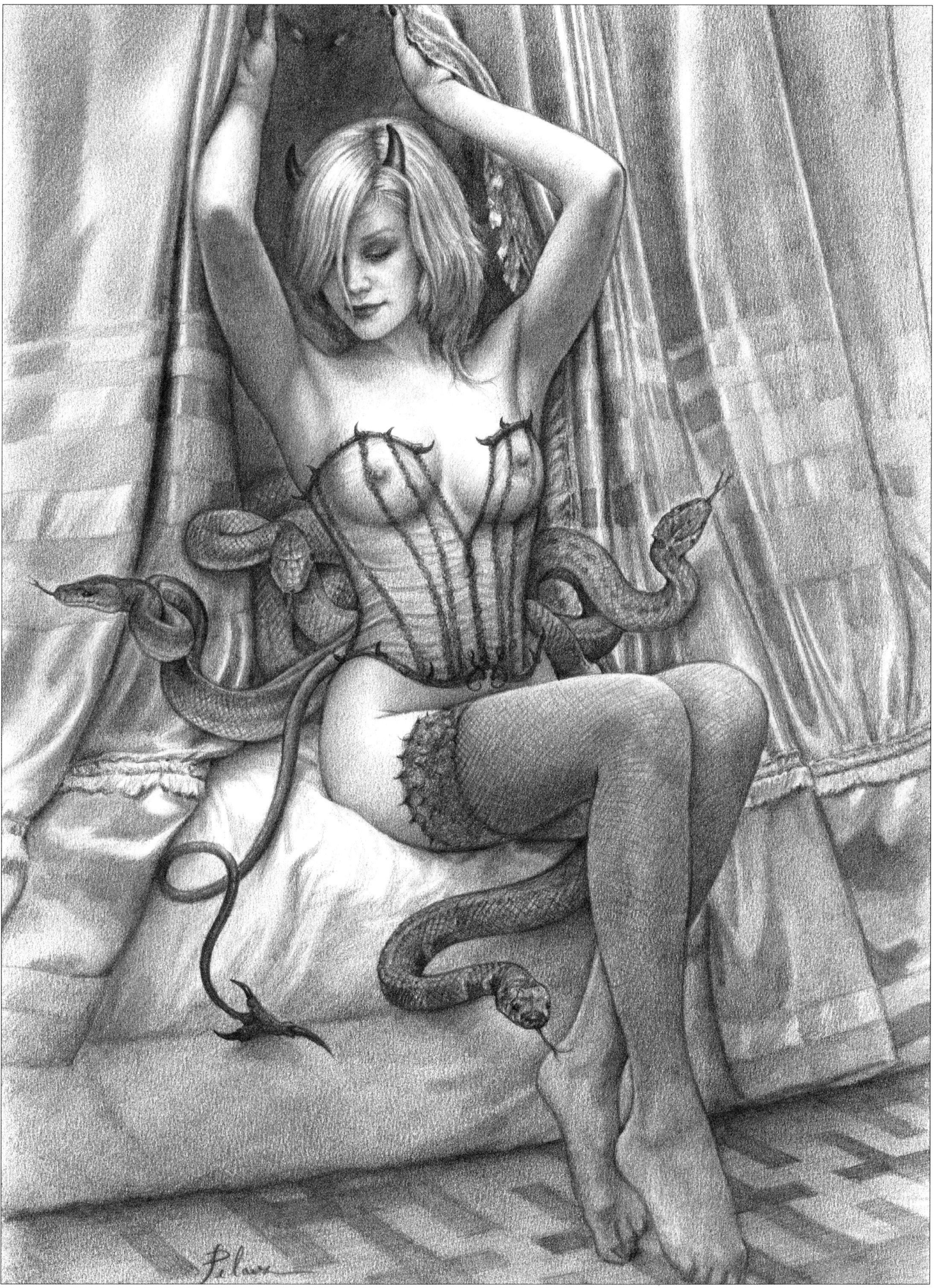

PELAEZ

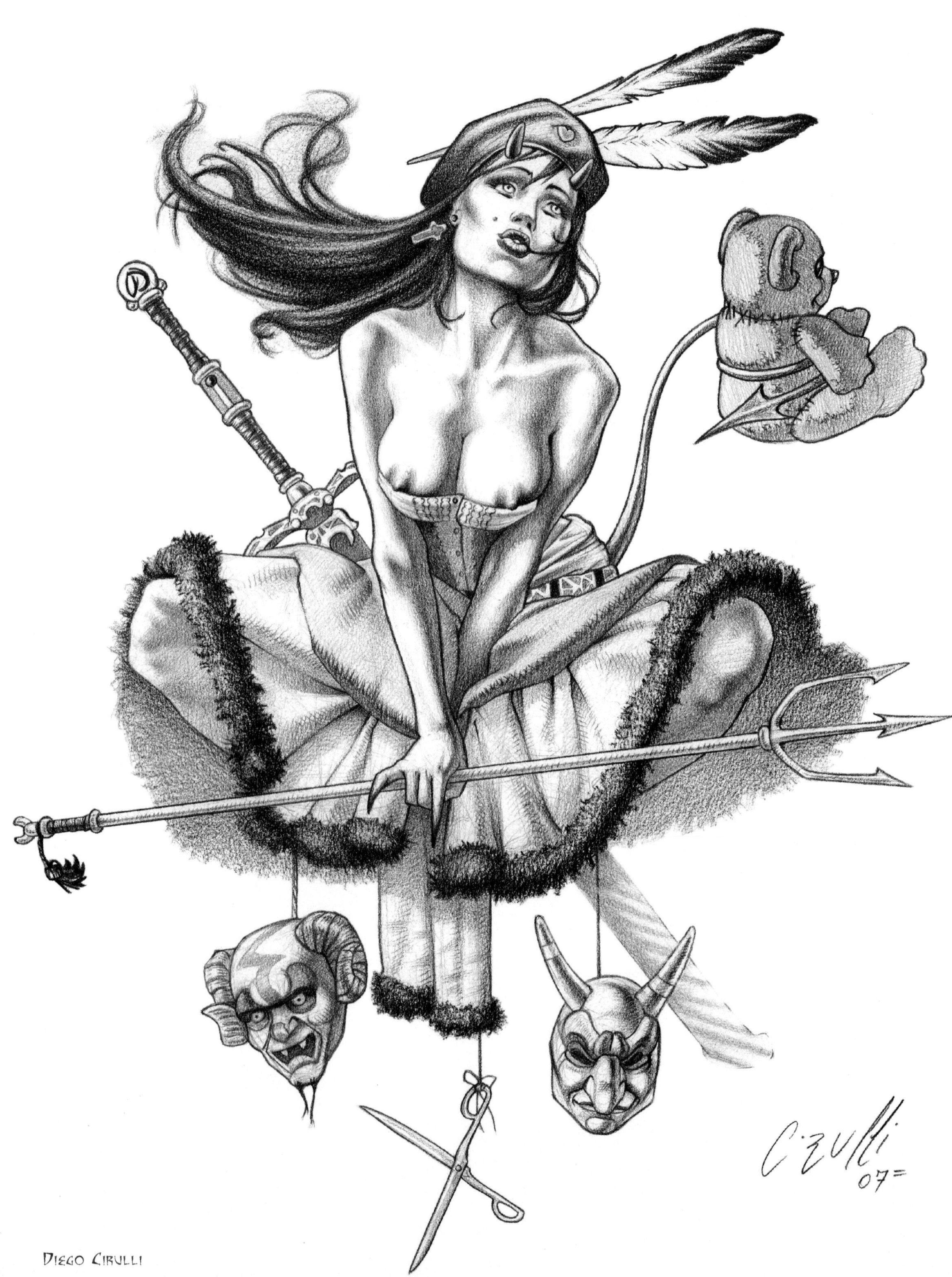

DIEGO CIRULLI

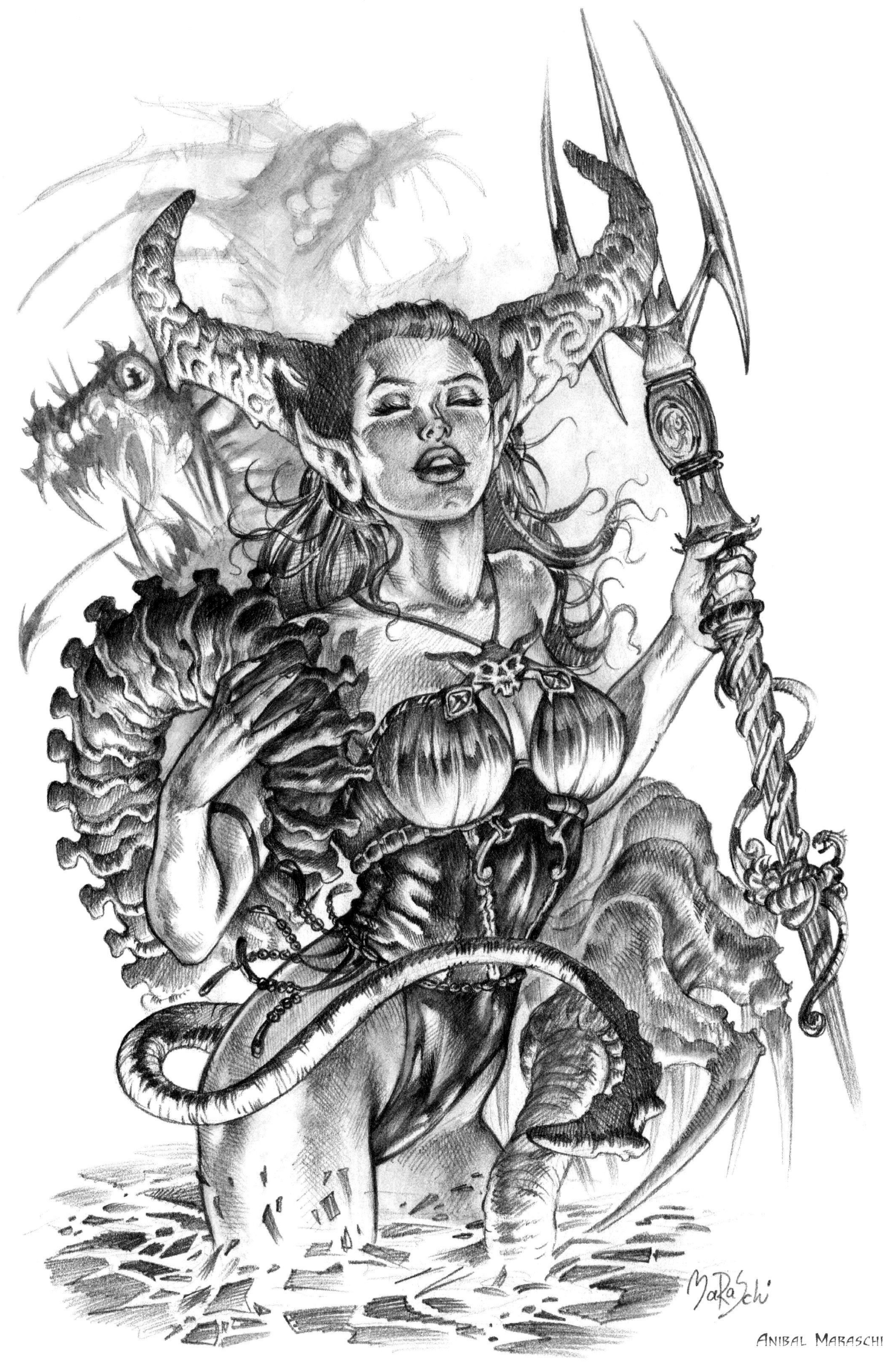
Anibal Maraschi

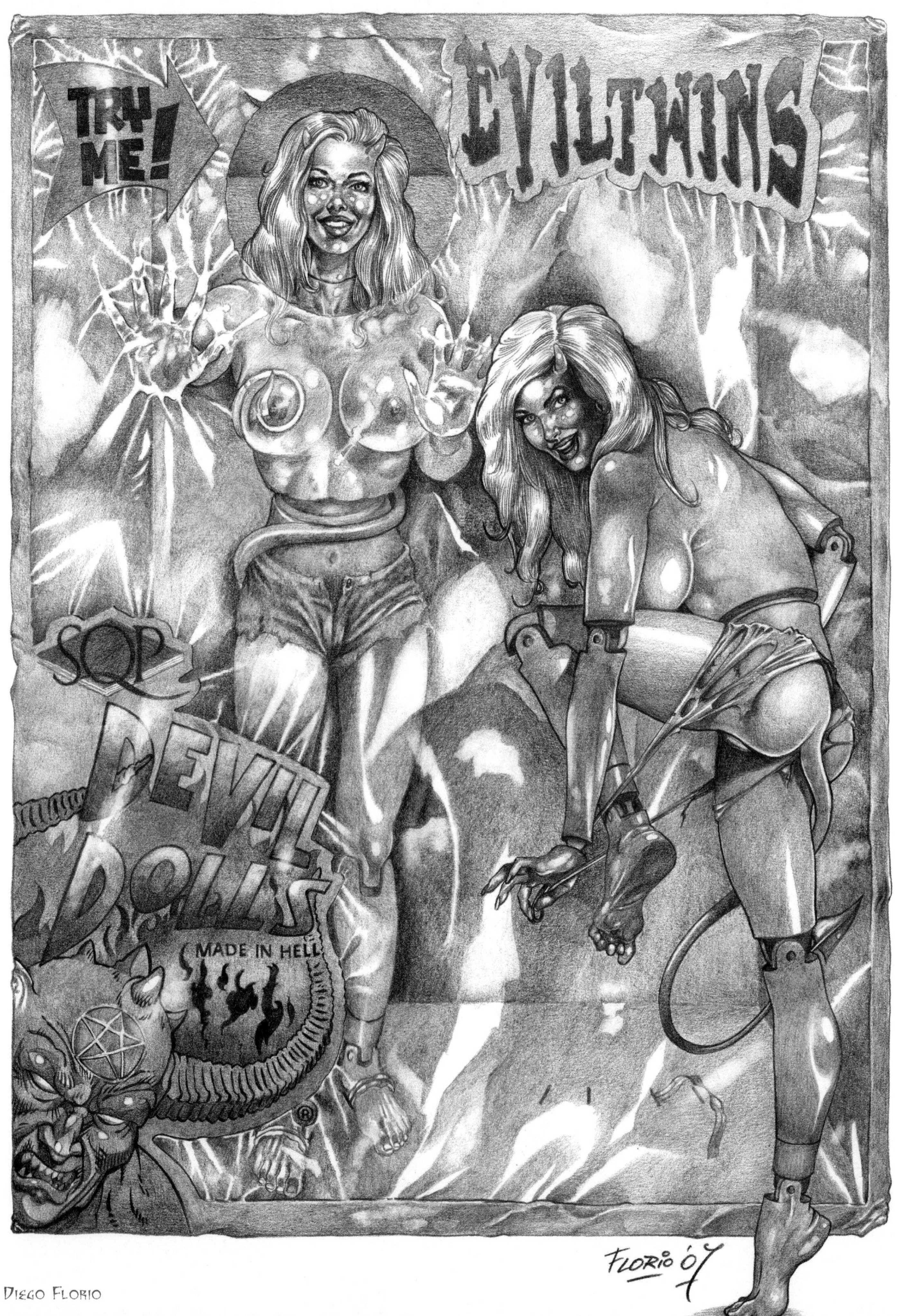

Diego Florio

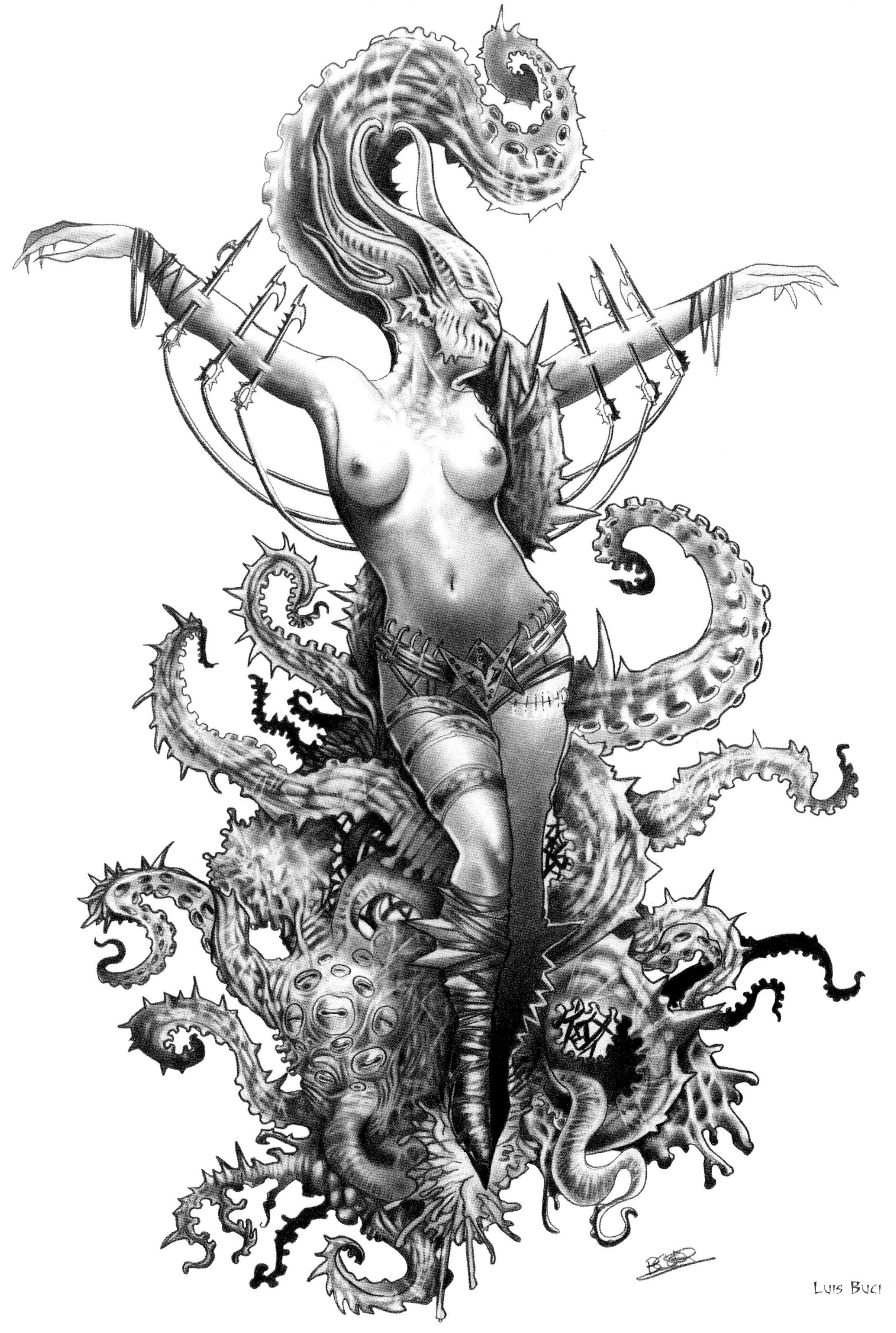

Luis Buci

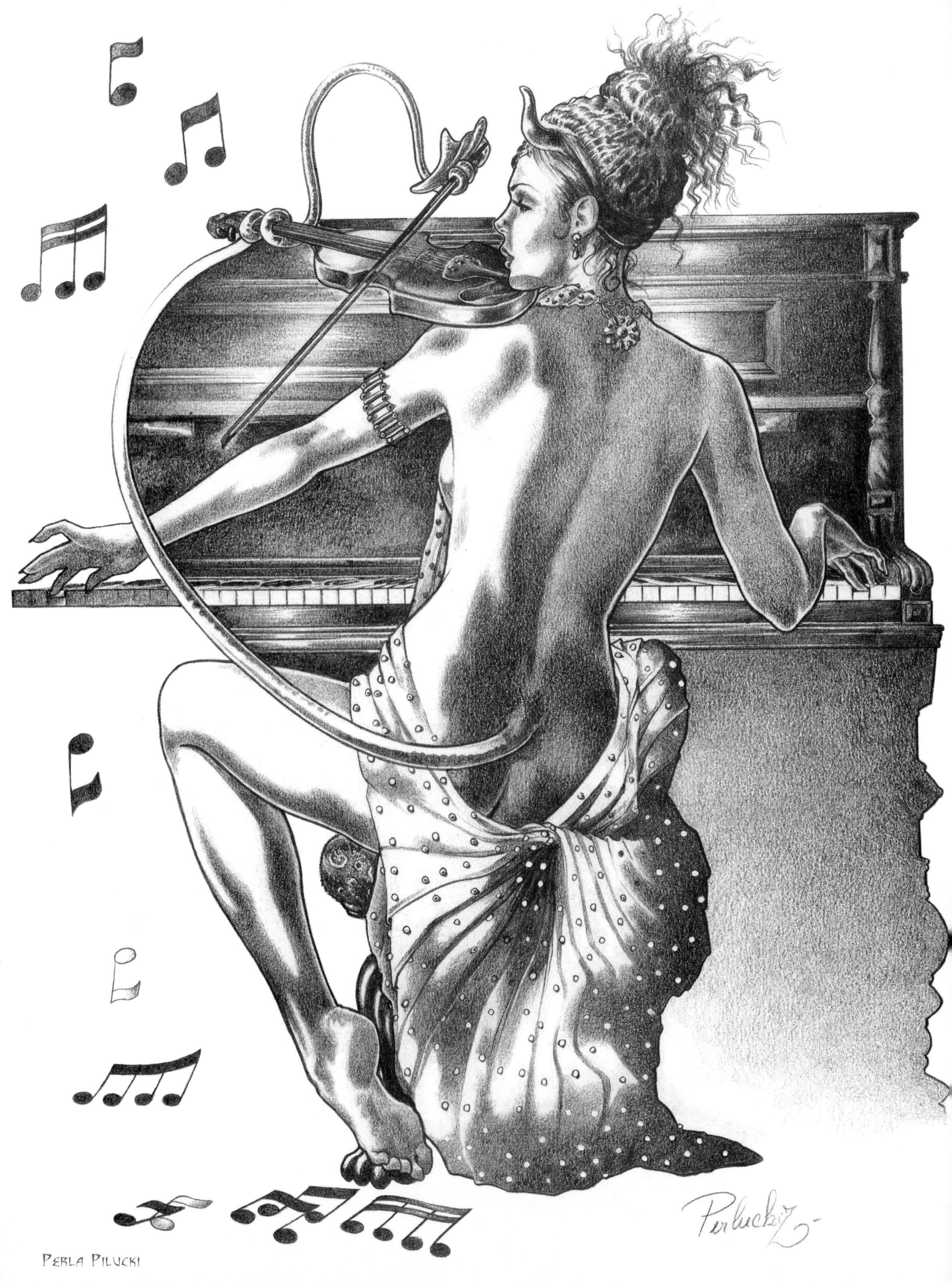
Perla Pilucki

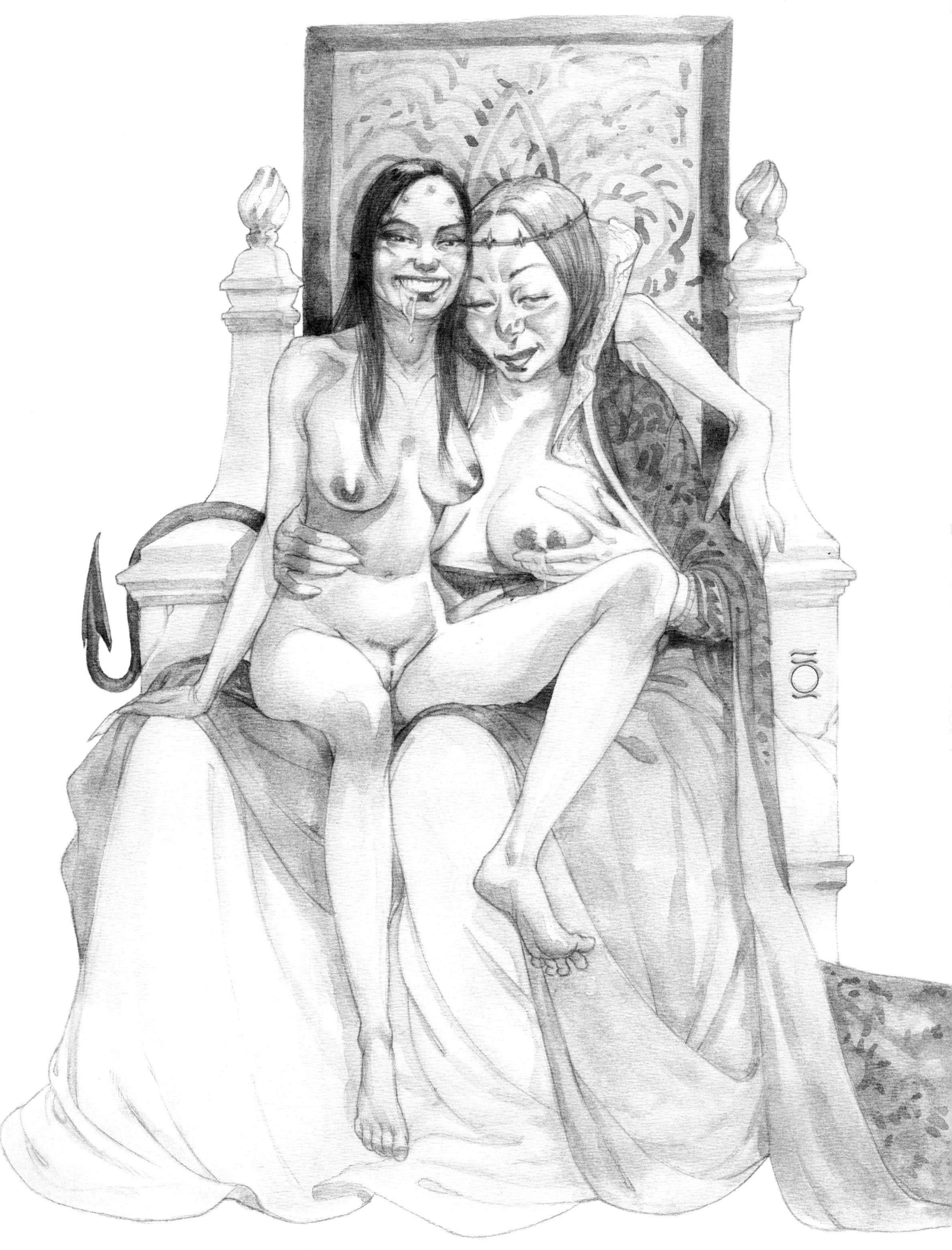

Marcelo Sosa.

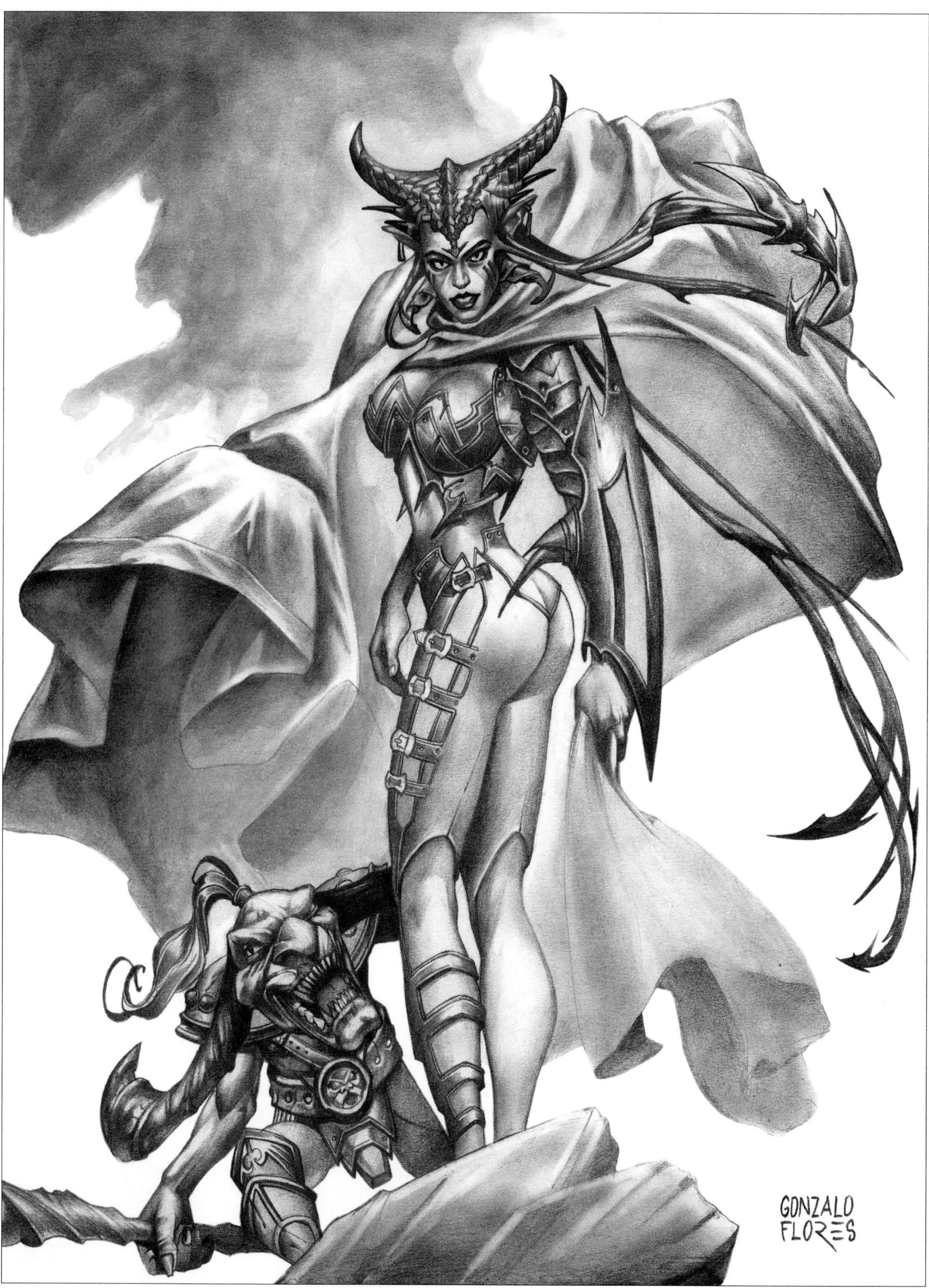

Gonzalo Flores

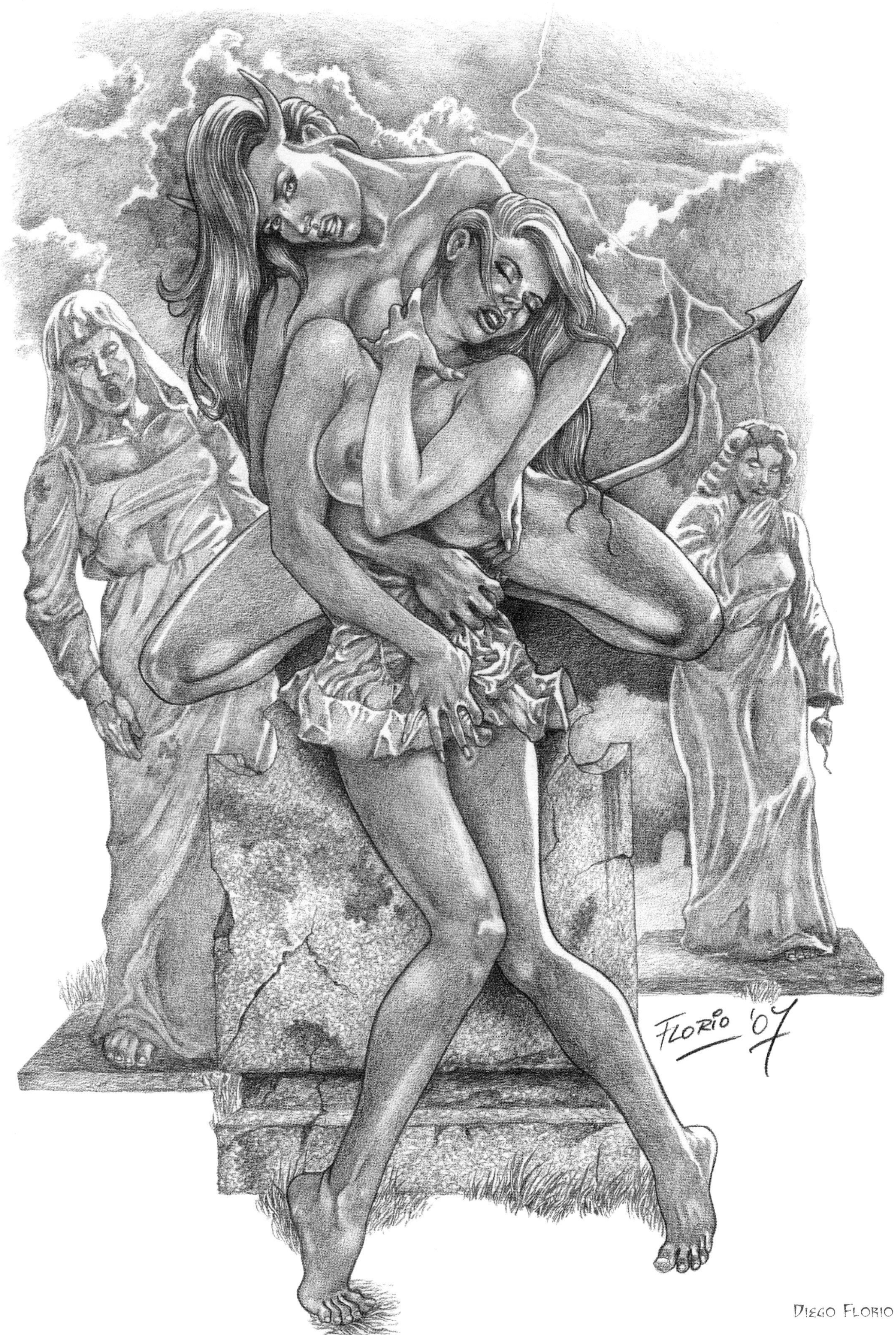
FLORIO '07
DIEGO FLORIO

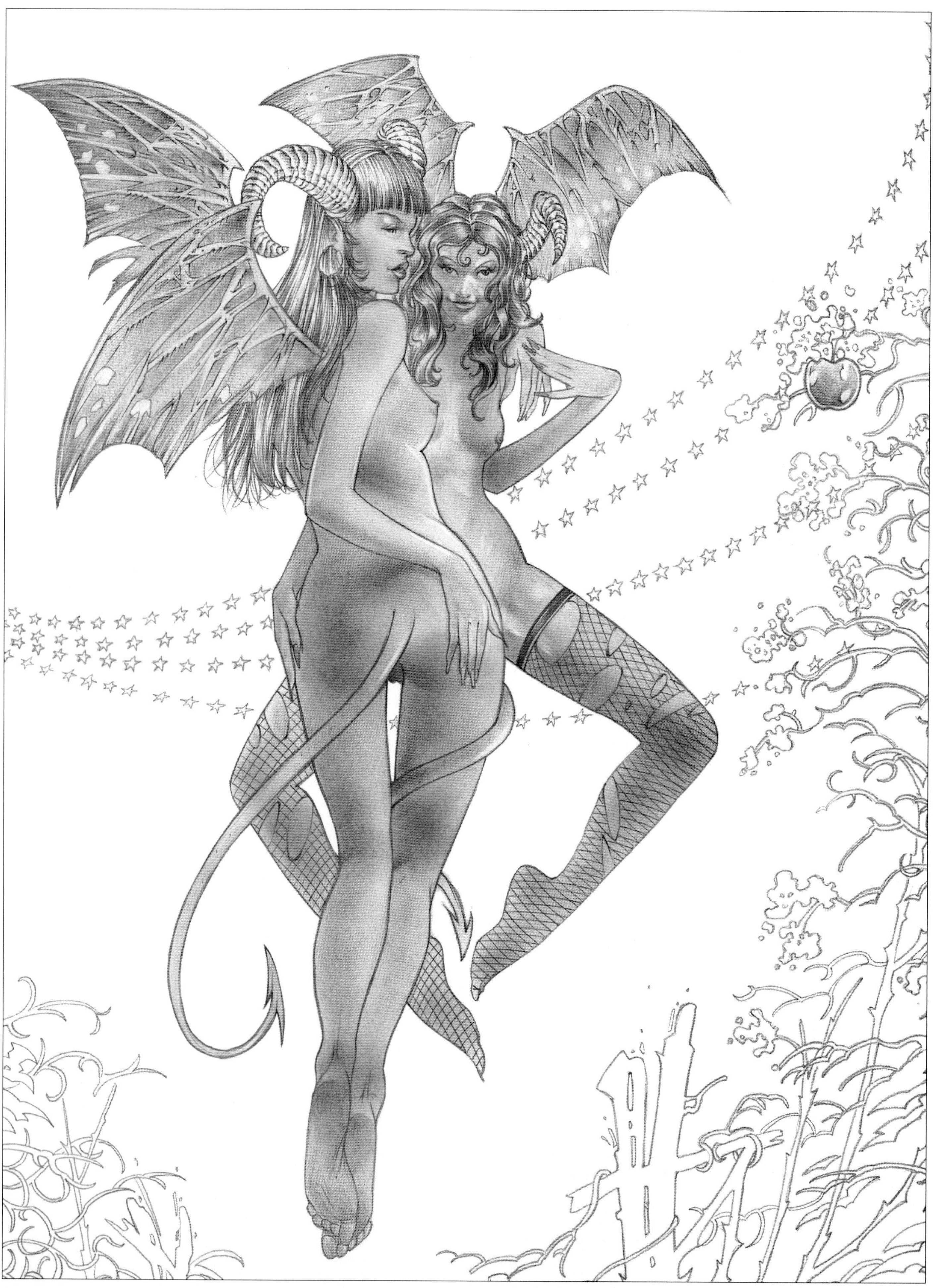

J.L. CZERNIAWSKI

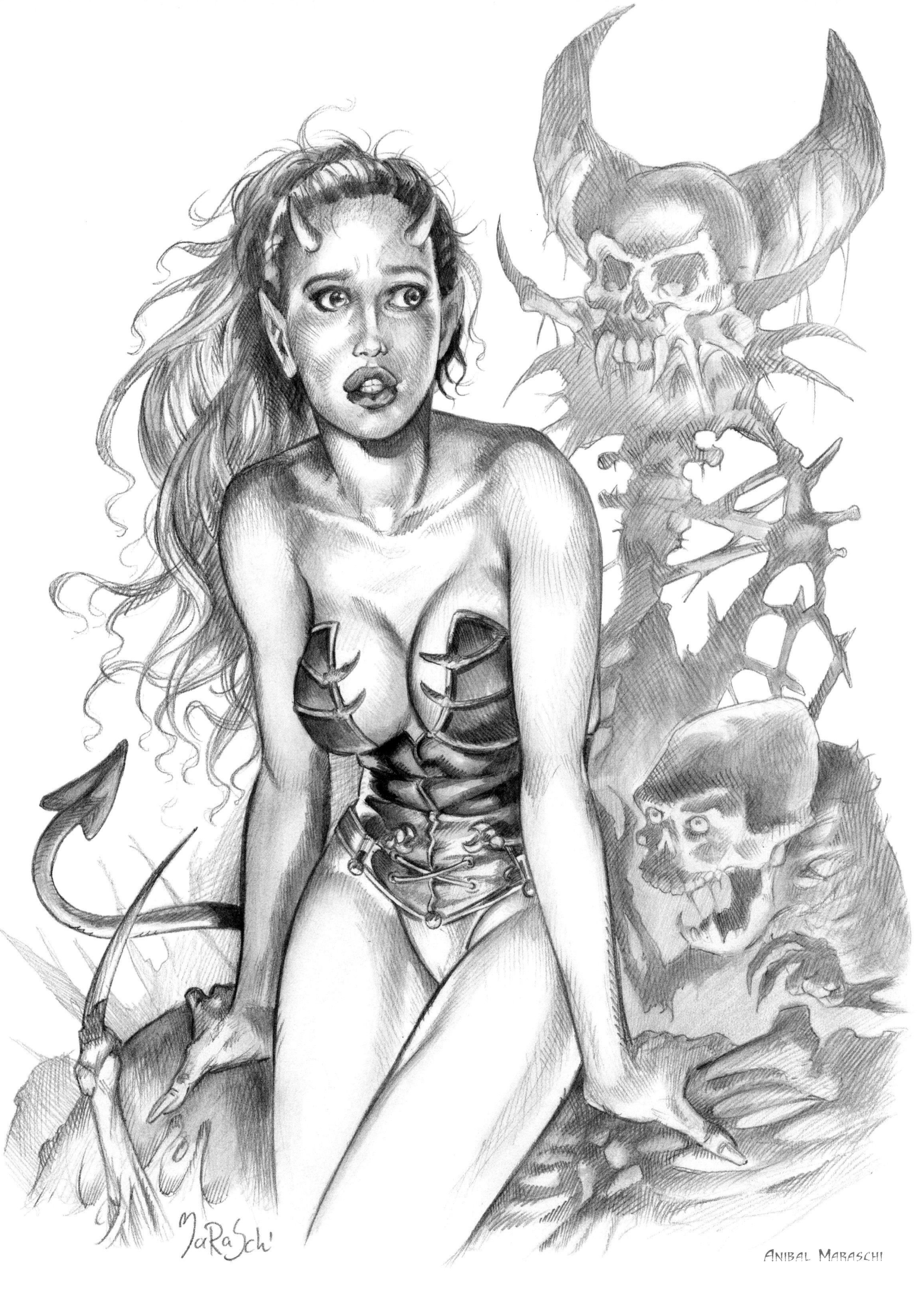
ANIBAL MARASCHI

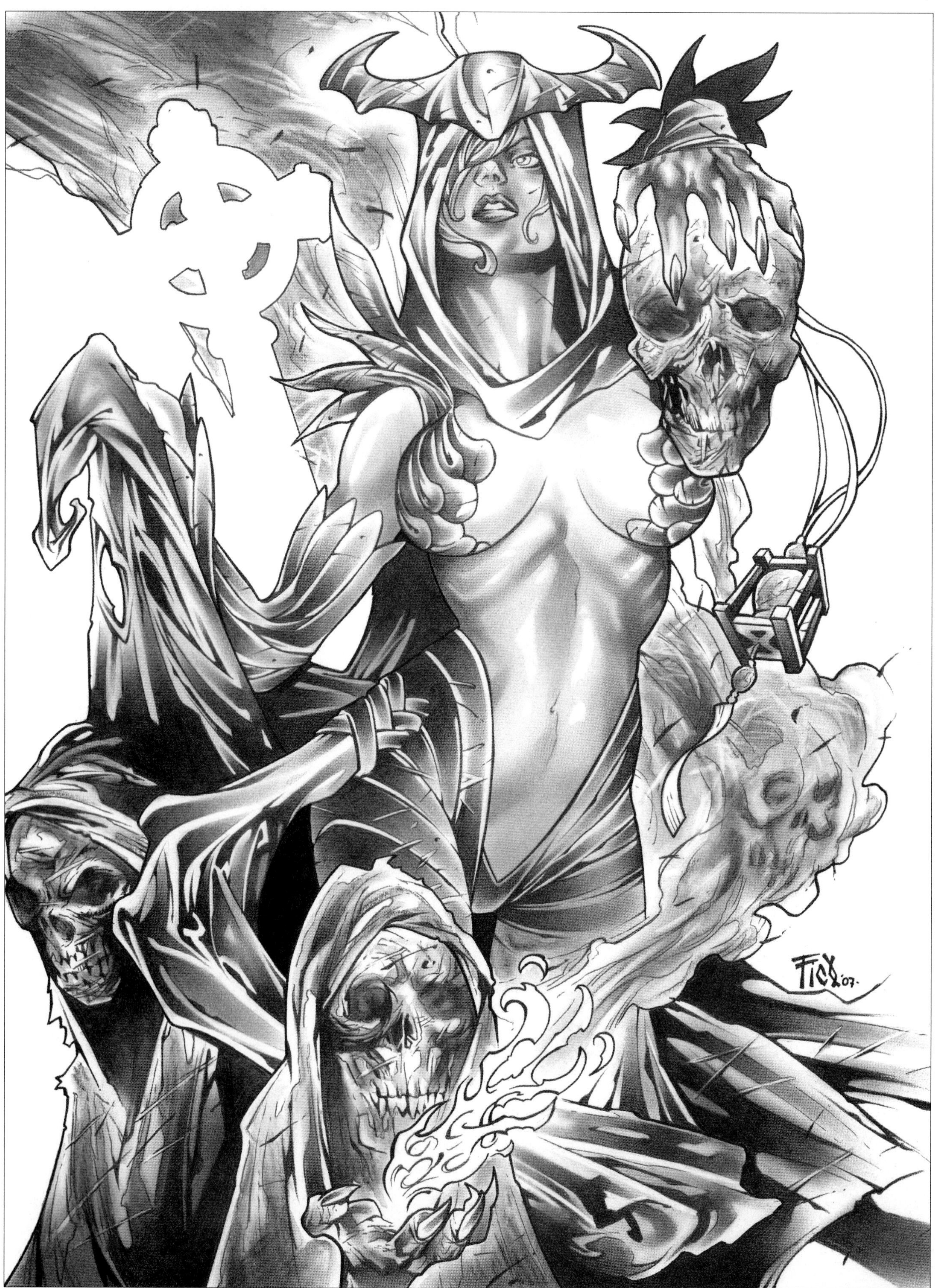

Federico Ossio

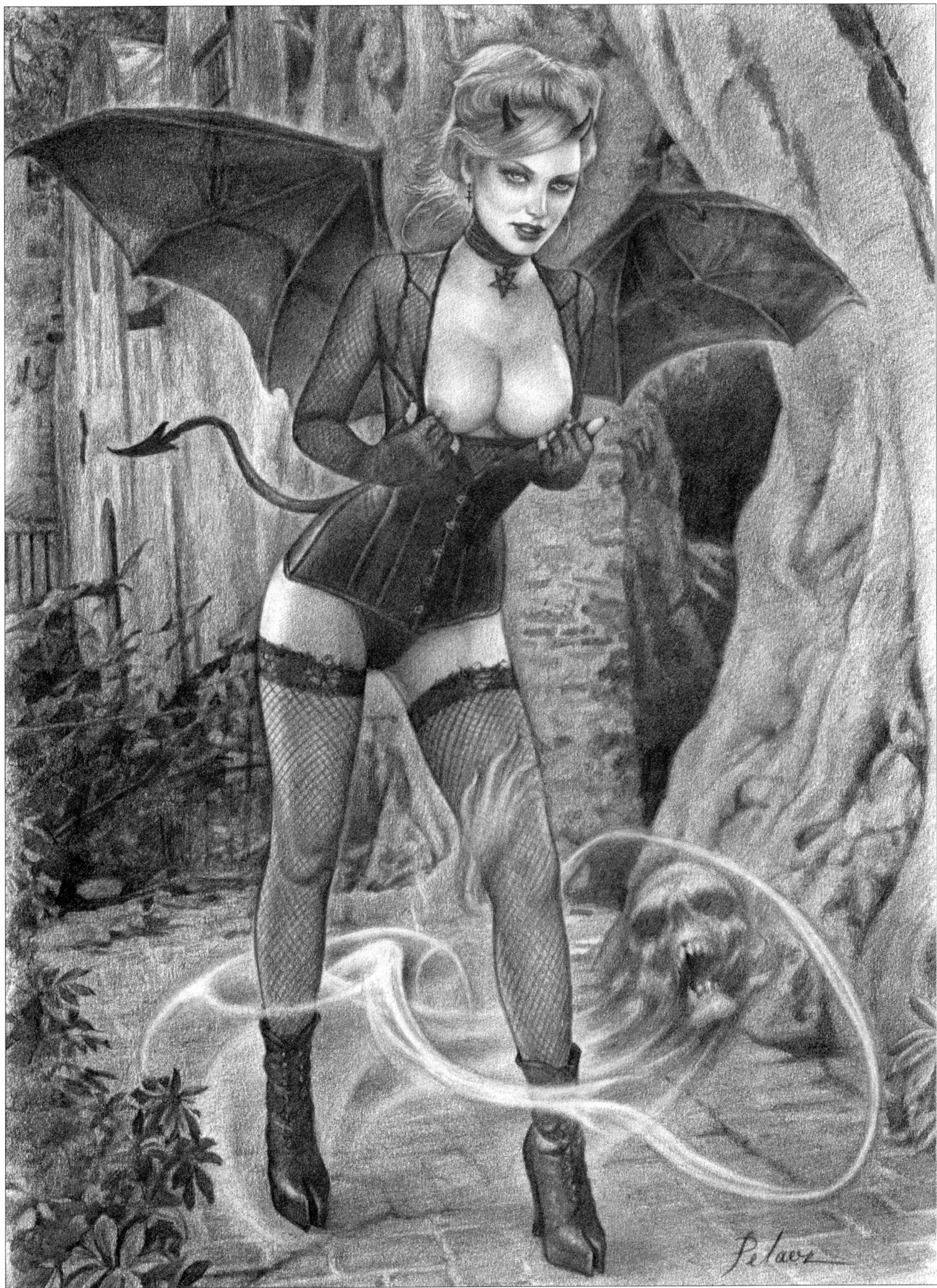

Pelaez

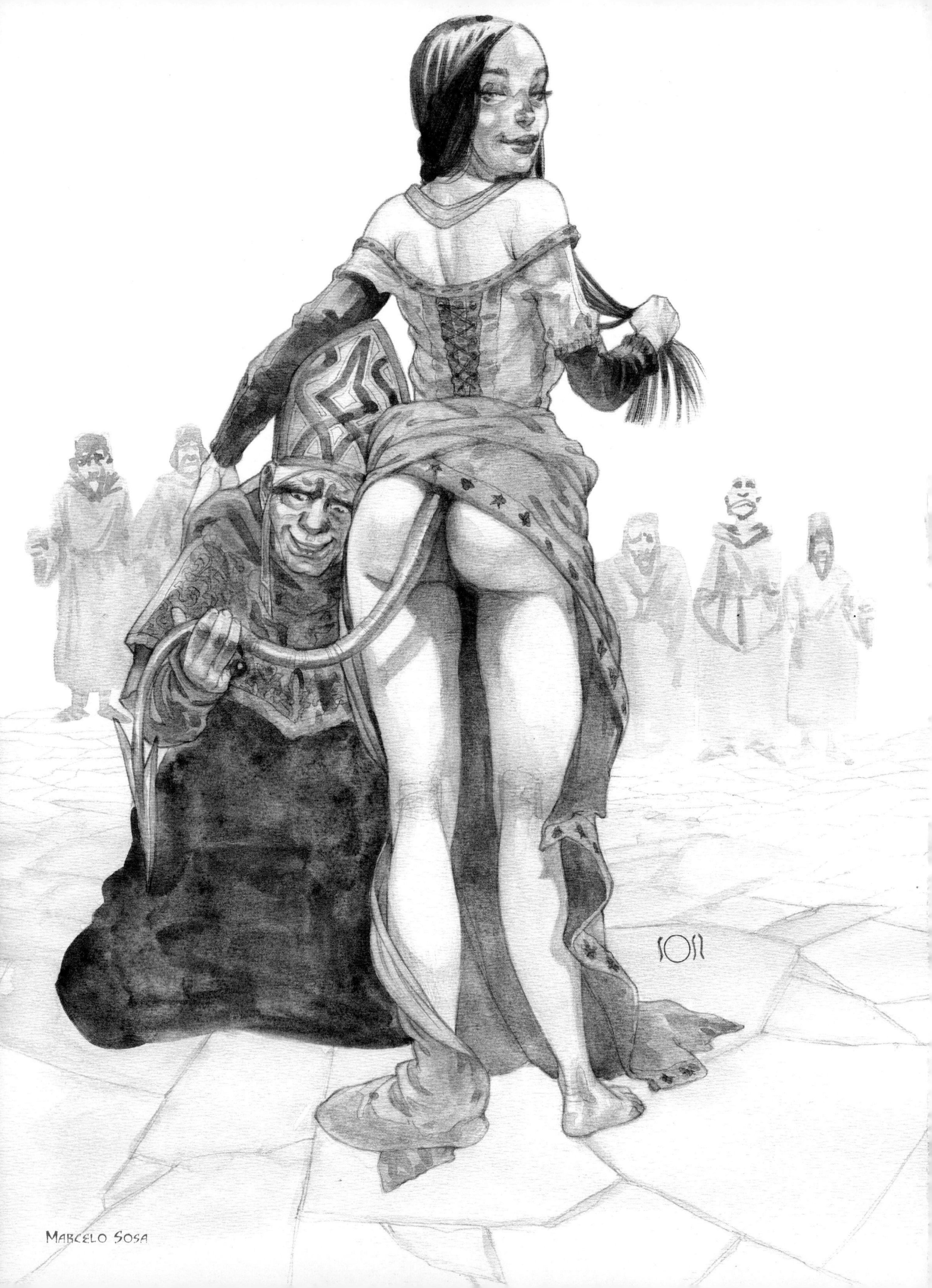
MARCELO SOSA